Losing Iraq

LOSING IRAQ

INSURGENCY AND POLITICS

Stephen C. Pelletière

PRAEGER SECURITY INTERNATIONAL
Westport, Connecticut • London

Library of Congress Cataloging-in-Publication Data

Pelletière, Stephen C.
    Losing Iraq : insurgency and politics / Stephen C. Pelletière.
        p. cm.
    Includes bibliographical references and index.
    ISBN-13: 978–0–275–99213–2 (alk. paper)
    1. Iraq War, 2003– 2. Insurgency—Iraq. 3. United States—Politics and government—2001–
I. Title.
    DS79.76.P354 2007
    956.7044'3–dc22   2007027870

British Library Cataloguing in Publication Data is available.

Library of Congress Catalog Card Number: 2007027870
ISBN-13: 978–0–275–99213–2

First published in 2007

Praeger Security International, 88 Post Road West, Westport, CT 06881
An imprint of Greenwood Publishing Group, Inc.
www.praeger.com

Printed in the United States of America

The paper used in this book complies with the
Permanent Paper Standard issued by the National
Information Standards Organization (Z39.48–1984).

10 9 8 7 6 5 4 3 2 1

To Jean

But he's dead, Signore, he's dead. Why not?

—Charles Dickens, *Pictures From Italy*

Contents

Acknowledgments

I would like to thank four people who have been helpful, supplying me with bits of wisdom and facts that I lacked: Pat Lang, Ken Katzman, Edmond Ghareeb, and Roger Trilling. Also I would like to thank my editors at Praeger, particularly Heather Staines. And I owe a debt of gratitude to the U.S. Army War College Library, its director Bodhan Kohutiak, and his staff for keeping me supplied with materials I needed to write this book and three previous ones on Iraq. Finally, to Neelo, my first reader, as always.

Introduction

Americans' attitudes towards the second Iraq War have taken an unhealthy course: a kind of obliviousness seems to have overcome many. To be sure most Americans pay lip service to fulfilling the mission but one senses that this is because the alternative, of cutting and running, is unacceptable, as things stand now.

A lot of the indifference is attributable, no doubt, to the way that news is disseminated in the media: with bulletins broadcast 24 hours around the clock, public affairs programming becomes like *Muzak,* mere background noise, something one need not pay attention to, much less be keenly involved with.

One can also get information about the war on the Web, but it is hard to tell whether it is reliable. Moreover it does seem that a lot of what is being conveyed there is opinionated and the opinion is not that of someone who knows.

What is needed is a book, not a big book, rather something on the order of an extended essay that would go into the matter of the war and the occupation and would try to explain the many contradictions that have grown up around it.

Much of what the Bush administration has been putting out about the war does not make sense. Consequently, Americans who may sincerely wish to understand their country's involvement find themselves at a loss: one will not keep up with the war if one's efforts to make sense of it continually are being frustrated. This is part of what I feel is causing Americans to turn off Iraq: the problems there do not seem to lend themselves to comprehension, much less resolution.

Take but one example of misapprehension: the Iraqi people supposedly are avid to begin life anew under a democracy. And yet the level of violence there has climbed steadily since "victory" was declared four years ago.

Bush tries to explain away this anomaly by claiming that those who oppose the American-backed government are "diehards," with no wide following in the society. They comprise, he claims, mainly ex-Ba'thists and religious warriors (so-called *jihadis*). Neither, the president says, is important. The ex-Ba'thists, according to Bush, are former officials of the old regime who fear that in any introduction of democracy to Iraq they will lose out. The jihadis are what Rumsfeld called nutters, fanatics, human flotsam from all over the Middle East, who have drifted up in Iraq to pursue a lost cause of trying to destroy Western civilization.

Two things about Bush's explanation do not track. The Ba'thists were not a large group to begin with: the Ba'th was ever a vanguard party, meaning its core membership was small. To be sure there were plenty of people who joined the party to advance their careers but such individuals never rose very far in its ranks; they tended to fill out the lower cadres. In any event, careerists would never fight as ferociously as do the resisters. True Ba'thists might, but (as I said) true Ba'thists represent a relatively small portion of the population. Then we have the jihadis. For all Bush's talk, the U.S. military has been unable to capture very many of these. So, if there are not a lot of committed ex-Ba'thists, and the jihadis are scarcely to be found, who is it that comprises the resistance? It is questions like this that this book sets out to answer.

I argue that America is operating in Iraq under a false flag. It claims that it is aiming to rebuild the country along the lines of a strong, cohesive nation/ state. But if that is what it is saying now, that was not the stated purpose when the war was declared. Before the war, Bush specifically disavowed nation-building. It was not until after the resistance commenced that administration figures began talking about committing resources to putting Iraq back together again, a simulacrum of what it was.

Moreover, if one skips what the Americans are *saying* to focus on what they are *doing,* the picture clouds up considerably. Many of the Americans' actions contradict their avowals. They support policies which, were they to be put into effect, would spell finis for Iraq as we know it.

For example, two Iraqi Shia leaders elevated by the Americans to high positions in the new government have been advocating a federal system whereby the southern, largely Shia portion of the country, would become autonomous. In the minds of many, this would translate into that area's being annexed by Iran. And in line with this, it is significant that *both these individuals fought on the side of Iran in the Iran-Iraq War (1980–1988).*

In a similar vein, America has lent its support to two Kurdish leaders who advocate creating a *separate Kurdish state* out of the North of Iraq. And these two—as was the case with the aforementioned Shias—fought on Iran's side in that war also.

Individuals such as these—and others whom I could mention, who simi-larly have found favor with the Americans—are at best lukewarm in their allegiance to Iraq, at worst, one feels, they are looking to break up the country.

I argue that it is suspicion of the Americans' motives that is fueling the current rebellion of Iraqis. I believe that quite a number of them have become convinced the United States is out to tear the state apart. To Americans, of course, such a conception is bizarre; they cannot conceive that the Bush administration, after having deposed the Ba'th, would seek to destroy Iraq, much less turn it over to the Iranians.

At the same time, there is a belief in the United States—widely held—that Iraq is not a real country; that it never really gelled as such. Consequently it is only half formed, an amalgam of ethnic groups—Shia, Sunni, and Kurdish—and that, since the natives have no concept of what it means to be an Iraqi, the disappearance of the entity that we now recognize as Iraq would pose no great loss.

One could argue that the Americans, whereas they may not actively be seeking the destruction of Iraq, would be prepared to countenance its disappearance by default.

I do not believe, *at all,* that Iraq is a failed state. However, I understand how so many in the United States might feel so—it is a matter of their being ignorant. Americans need to be educated about what went on in Iraq under the Ba'th, or at least in the period while Saddam Hussein was in charge there. The Iraqi leader came to power in 1979. Almost immediately after taking the reins of government he led his country to war with Iran, and it is that episode that is vital to know about, otherwise very little of what is going on now in Iraq can be made sense of.

The Iran-Iraq War was the longest conventional armed combat post-World War II; it was also one of the bloodiest. Both sides in that war are supposed to have lost hundreds of thousands *each.*[1] I argue in this book that the experience of waging what essentially was an existential struggle, against a foe who for centuries had been aggressing against Iraq changed the Iraqis.[2] The war gave them an identity that they had not possessed before, and the confidence to assert their identity in military acts.

Also in line with this, I am going to argue that, with the successful conclusion of the Iran-Iraq War, the Ba'th legitimized its rule over the country: it met the three requirements of a successful regime: it showed that it could govern; could sustain itself, and could defend the country against external aggression.[3] Under my construction, the belief of Americans that the Ba'th constituted a collection of thugs, holding on to power by coercive means, does not stand to reason. In any event, I think this is the basis of much of the difficulty America is experiencing now with the Iraqis in trying to rule them: they mistake the nature of the people with whom they are having to deal.

I just said that the Iran-Iraq War ended with a great upset, the Iraqis not having been tipped to win it. Indeed throughout the war they were accounted the underdogs. I would say that for the first three years of the war the Iraqis essentially were floundering; yet they pulled themselves up, and in the fourth year—after an initial severe setback—slowly commenced to grind the Iranians down, and then in the eighth year came the bravura finish that took the world so by surprise. The credit for this turnaround must go to the Iraqi army which, to bring it off, had first to reconstitute itself. Among lesser ranked armies one usually does not see an effort on such a scale succeed, not as spectacularly as did this. At the end of the war the officers responsible for the great victory had cause to be proud, and most certainly they had a sense of themselves as professionals. Then came the United States and stripped them of what they deemed was their earned reward, by—as I will explain in the second chapter—taking the Iranians' side to prevent the Iraqis from imposing a victor's peace.

Actually the United States went farther: it not only sabotaged the negotiations for a peace that would have aggrandized Iraq, it set the country back in its development at least a couple of decades. With its wholesale bombing of Iraqi cities (in the first Iraq War), the Americans blasted the country's infrastructure, which meant that it could not recover from the devastation of the just-concluded conflict with Iran. And then the United States and Britain saddled Iraq with the most Draconian sanctions imposed on a people in the post-World War II era.

But what to the Iraqis was most affronting (I feel) were the enactments laid on by the occupiers after the Americans won the second Iraq War: these measures were perceived by Iraqis as ruinous.

In one of their very first decrees on taking over in Iraq, the Americans ordered the Iraqi army and police disbanded. This immediately put thousands of officers out of work and drove many (we must assume) into the arms of the resistance. Next, L. Paul Bremer III, America's proconsul, issued a decree barring ex-Ba'thists from serving in the postwar government. If the Iraqis had suspicions about the Americans' trustworthiness, these moves of Bremer confirmed them. For how else does one explain the dismantling of the very institutions—the army, the police, and Ba'th Party—on which Iraqis had come to depend for their survival? These outfits sustained the country through three wars and the difficult period of the UN-imposed sanctions. How do you rebuild the country (as Americans were claiming they were going to do) if you start by cashiering the only truly competent people, in effect turning them into outlaws?

In any event, this is an indication of the approach I take. In the first chapter I will look at the invasion and Iraq's response to it, which so confounded the Americans. The Iraqi army fought, with surprising effectiveness. Further, the Shias in the cities of the South, whom the Americans had expected to come over to them, fought alongside the Iraqi army. In the second chapter I give a brief history of the Iraqi army, focusing on the period of the 1980s and the Iran-Iraq War. I argue that this war transformed the army, a change which largely escaped the notice of the United States. In Chapter 3 I discuss American intelligence about Iraq on the eve of the war; characterize it as delusory; and show that, once inside Iraq (after the successful invasion) the intelligence did not improve, which led to the deterioration of relations with the Iraqis, and precipitated the revolt that is currently going on. In Chapter 4 I discuss the clash between the so-called expatriates and native Iraqis, and the part the Islamic Republic is playing under the occupation.

Overall, I show that the actions taken by the Americans contradict avowals of what they supposedly had come to Iraq to accomplish.

This latter argument begs a very large question: What in fact are the Americans aiming for? If they are not trying to rebuild Iraq—as they maintain—what are they after? And, here I try—in the analysis portion of this study—to relate the Americans' behavior in Iraq to the wider sphere of U.S. interests in the Persian Gulf and beyond to all of the Middle East. This war in Iraq is an affair of much greater purport than Western observers have so far been willing to admit.

I connect the war to what is presently occurring in Lebanon and to the much older and much more bitterly contested insurrection of the Palestinians in the Occupied Territories.

In my view, the second Iraq War is not a civil war, it is not a religious war, it is rather part of a larger geopolitical struggle that encompasses not just the Iraqis or the Iranians, but the Israelis and all of the other client states of the United States in the Middle East. In other words, it involves the whole network of alliances that Washington forged during the years of the Cold War.

Americans might want to consider that this war is only the first of what will play out as a series of struggles, the aim of which is to preserve the client system of the old Cold War days.

1

The Invasion Phase

The war got off to a bad start with an ill-fated expedition by Paul Wolfowitz to Ankara. America's deputy secretary of defense (and one of the architects of the war) seems to have believed that he could coerce the Turks. Before he left for Ankara (on December 1, 2002) Wolfowitz stated publicly he was going abroad to finalize arrangements for American forces to open a second front against Iraq from Turkey's southeast.[1] The Turks for weeks had been saying that they *would not* approve an invasion of Iraq from Turkey. The government of Recip Tayyip Erdogan had just been elected; the election had been a close one and the new prime minister did not have a secure mandate.[2] Public opinion in Turkey was against the war; it certainly opposed having the Americans open a second front against Iraq from Turkish soil.

Wolfowitz evidently was persuaded that by going personally to Turkey he could overcome the Turks' objections. After all here was a representative of the world's most powerful nation—and Turkey's most important ally—*in Ankara,* making an appeal for support. Could Erdogan turn him down? Would he not be ashamed (perhaps even a little fearful) to do so?

Erdogan was not, and he did. Wolfowitz kept his cool; he made no intemperate remarks (that came later).[3] Most immediately the Americans were counting on a reversal: they hoped that Turkey's parliament would vote to overrule Erdogan. However, the parliament delayed and delayed until early March 2003 before taking up the Americans' request and then it supported the turndown.

This effectively left the Americans out on the end of a very long limb. The original war plan, as conceived by the U.S. Defense Department, envisioned a two-pronged attack on Iraq—one from the North in Turkey, another from the South in Kuwait. In preparation for the northern thrust, the Americans had positioned the U.S. Fourth Infantry Division on a flotilla of over 40 ships in the Mediterranean. They had some 40,000 soldiers, plus heavy tanks and equipment, anchored off Turkey's southern coast, waiting to go ashore—*and now what?*

The division had to sail away. It had to make the journey across the Mediterranean; pass through the Suez Canal; go down the Red Sea Coast; up around the Arabian peninsula to Kuwait. Given that the Americans had waited until the last possible minute to haul anchor, the Fourth could not possibly arrive in time for the invasion, were it to go ahead as planned.[4]

There was to be no delay; Bush did not amend the war plan in the face of this so considerable reversal. Indeed he actually speeded it up. General Tommy Franks (the Allies' supreme commander) had originally planned to kick off the war with a week-long air attack, targeting Baghdad and other sites around Iraq. However, the night of March 19, George Tenet, director of the Central Intelligence Agency (CIA), got a tip that Saddam Hussein and a number of top Ba'thists were in a bunker in Baghdad. Tenet took the information to Defense Secretary Donald Rumsfeld and his deputy, Wolfowitz, and then, after passing it to the president, it was decided to drop a 2,000-pound bomb on the bunker, the idea being to zap the Ba'thist leadership, crippling the Iraqis' command structure all at a go, so to speak.[5]

The intelligence was wrong (unfortunately for the Americans). Even so, that should not have stopped Franks from proceeding with his plan; that is, with the week-long softening-up raids by the U.S. Air Force. However, he changed things around. Instead of having the Air Force lead off, with the ground forces only going into Iraq after a week, now the ground forces attacked straightaway, no softening-up raids, no preliminaries. To be sure the Air Force did bomb. It is estimated that on the first day of the war it dropped over a thousand precision-guided missiles and bombs—of all sizes—on Baghdad.[6] But this was done coincidentally with the ground forces going in.

There is something troubling about this switch of Franks. His explanation of why he did it does not make a lot of sense. He said he wanted to achieve the element of surprise.[7] But *how so?* The Iraqis certainly knew the Americans were coming; it is unlikely that Hussein and the top Ba'thists hoped for a reprieve, to dodge the bullet, as we say.[8]

So how was sending ground forces into Iraq precipitously achieving surprise? I do not think it was. I think we have to look farther for an explanation. The Americans had been receiving reports that the oil fields were imperiled; that the Ba'thists intended to torch them. By rushing in, the Americans may have hoped to forestall that eventuality.[9] This is a plausible explanation. However, if this was their intent, they would not have been likely to own up to it. The Americans were aware that, in the eyes of much of the world, they were invading to get their hands on Iraq's oil, and therefore they went out of their way not to make it appear that they were primarily focused on seizing the fields.[10]

There is another explanation for the decision to change plans; that is that Bush and his circle really did believe the Iraqis were going to greet them as liberators, throw flower petals in their path, as neo-con Kanan Makiya had said.[11] They may have envisioned the invasion as a kind of triumphal march, with little or no opposition. In that case, why bomb? Spare the infrastructure, which the Americans would need to facilitate the running of the country in the occupation phase.

In any event, the decision to speed things up was almost certainly not Franks's—it was more likely taken by Bush's inner circle, and most notably (one guesses) by Rumsfeld. Donald Rumsfeld, the U.S. defense secretary, was a take-charge kind of guy, as we say, and he micromanaged the war at every stage. Along with that, the secretary—who over the years had cultivated a reputation of being a risk taker—espoused the so-called air war strategy (more about which later).[12] He held no brief for the doctrine of overwhelming force, which Secretary of State Colin Powell had promulgated when he was head of the Joint Chiefs of Staff, and to which the U.S. Army subscribed (and to which it still subscribes).[13] Rumsfeld believed in keeping ground troops to a minimum; in fact, he was all for showcasing Special Operations forces—to the detriment of more traditional combat entities.

Taking all this into account, it is difficult not to conclude that Rumsfeld was grandstanding. It is also possible to conjecture that he was afraid of drawing attention to his gaffe with the Turks. By waiting for the Fourth Division to arrive in Kuwait, Rumsfeld would have been admitting he had miscalculated there. Someone as prone to preen as was Rumsfeld would never have wanted to do that.

At the same time, these early moves on the part of the Americans underscore a fact about the war: there does not seem to have been any method as to what the civilians planning the war were doing. Here, in short order, we see them first try to strong-arm Turkey into, in effect, becoming an accomplice to the aggression; then they turn the invasion plan around, jump starting it by dropping a bunker-busting bomb on Baghdad; and then they push the ground forces into combat before the enemy has been softened up with air raiding. Finally, they override the generals, who were pleading with the administration to go slow and wait for the Fourth Division to arrive.[14] Bush and his people seem to have been trying out approaches, on a whim almost: *Hey, let's bomb the Ba'thist leadership; hey, what'd you say we turn the war plan around and go straight on in with ground troops?*

As for actual conditions on the ground, they do not appear to have given those much thought.[15]

Over the course of the book I will point out other similar instances of, let us call it, ill-advised behavior on the part of the Bush administration in regard to the conduct of the war (and of the occupation). This was a war like no other the United States fought, inasmuch as decisions affecting it seemed regularly to come from within a small, tight circle of *civilians* around the president, a circle which, one could say, was hermetically sealed; the generals were left out—compulsorily kept so, one feels.

The ground attack went operational the night of March 20. At 3 a.m., the first, second, and third brigades of the U.S. Army's Third Infantry Division and the First Marine Expeditionary Force rolled forward into Iraq, crossing the border from Kuwait. Before they did, however, a way had to be cleared for them. The Iraqis had erected as obstacles huge sand berms along the Kuwait frontier. These were hosed down with a specially provided water cannon. Razor-like jets cut through the berms, carving wide channels through which the Americans (and the British) could pass.

The plan was for the three army brigades to dash up the west bank of the Euphrates River, through the desert, bypassing the cities of Nasiriyah, Samawah, and Najaf, all of which lay to the East.[16] President Bush described the maneuver in a speech he gave to an audience at Camp Lejeune, North Carolina: "Our destination is Baghdad. We will accept nothing less than complete and final victory."[17]

In other words the Americans would not be diverted; they would go right for the jugular, the jugular in this case being Hussein and the Ba'thist leadership lodged in the capital. There may have been another reason for adopting the bypass strategy: the cities being passed were all Shia, and, in the Americans' view, the Shias were an oppressed community in Iraq. Indeed the Americans expected the Shias to revolt and open up their cities to them. Under such circumstances there would have been no reason to go in: the cities would capitulate as soon as the invasion commenced.

This, as we will see, was not a warranted assumption. However, it was not the only misapprehension the Americans labored under. They also believed that they had suborned a number of key Iraqi commanders who would lay down their arms. Coming over to the Allied side, the commanders would bring their units with them. This, too, never happened.[18]

With such false assumptions it is no wonder that the invasion, before it had proceeded too far along, began showing signs that it would miscarry. The first hint of trouble came the very first day, practically. The Iraqi 51st Mechanized Division (also referred to in the reporting as the 51st Regular Army Division), was one of those that the Americans believed they had suborned; they were counting on it to come over, which it was initially reported to have done; but these reports proved spurious as the 51st subsequently showed up inside Basrah where it put up a stubborn defense for as long as the war lasted.[19] The failure of the 51st to surrender was particularly disappointing because this was a *regular* army unit (not one of the elite Republican Guard outfits). Hussein had treated the regulars badly in the first Iraq War, which had led the Americans to believe that the regulars would surrender.[20] There was another cause for disappointment: the Americans believed that the regulars were all Shias, and that it was the elite units, the Republican Guards, who were predominantly Sunni.[21] Thus the fact of this regular army unit choosing to fight clashed with the Americans' view of how the war would go. That Shias would fight for the regime was not something they had considered.

U.S. Marine units had also been detailed off to seize Umm Qasr, Iraq's only working port on the Gulf. Its capture was deemed crucial. The Americans intended not only to funnel supplies through the port to their frontline fighters, but also they aimed to bring in humanitarian relief for the Iraqis through the port once victory was declared.[22] In the American camp, jubilation greeted the report on March 22 of Umm Qasr's fall.[23] Then, two days later, reporters embedded with the Marines noted continued fighting in and around the port area.

To those in Washington who from the first had been cautioning against optimism, the fightback of the Iraqis at Umm Qasr appeared ominous. That resistance should develop so soon, *and that it should show up so far south (on the very border with Kuwait!)* was portentous, they felt.

Something else was of concern: Who were these holdout fighters? They did not appear to be from regular Iraqi army units; at least, they were not wearing uniforms. The initial reports from the White House described them as "death squads," comprising diehard loyalists of the Ba'th regime.[24] General Franks's command in Qatar picked up this line, declaring that "dead enders," knowing their doom was sealed, were vainly striving to delay the inevitable.

The first, second, and third brigades of the Third Division pushed on at an astonishing rate of speed up along the west bank of the Euphrates. In two days some vanguard units were a third of the way to Baghdad, and it was predicted that, going at this rate, they would be at the capital, Baghdad, in a day or two.[25] *The Washington Post* claimed that this was one for the books: no modern mechanized column had ever, under combat conditions, moved so far so fast.[26]

Meanwhile, the British, the Americans' firm allies, also were on the move. The British were focused on Basrah, which—as with Nasiriyah, Samawah, and Najaf—was virtually 100 percent Shia. The British did not believe that they would have to fight for Basrah. Like the Americans, they felt that, because Basrah was so overwhelmingly Shia, the city would surrender to them.[27] The British plan was to besiege Basrah and wait for the *Basrawis* to initiate a revolt, at which point they would go in and assist them.

However, like Umm Qasr, things in Basrah did not work out as planned. On the circumference of the city, the Iraqis erected a line of defense behind which they blazed away at the invaders. Indeed some Iraqi defenders actually made sallies out of the city, to strike at the besieging British forces.[28] And again the question arose, *who were these "fanatics?"* (It is worth noting how the terminology employed by the British, as well as the

Americans, tended towards the psychological: "fanatics" implies deranged individuals, creatures outside the norm, as of course does the term "death squads"). According to the British, fanatical Ba'thists, having cowed the local population (all 1.5 million of them), were putting up a desperate last ditch fight, while at the same time they were preventing the Basrawis from rising.[29]

In any event, the British move on Basrah had stalled. But then so had the Americans' push towards Baghdad. Five days into the war and Umm Qasr was still being contested. This meant that supplies essential to the column of Americans speeding north were not getting into Iraq, much less moving up country to where the attack was spearheaded. American reporters began referring to Umm Qasr as an outpost of resistance.

It is a part of military doctrine that, when conducting a deep penetration like this, one does not want to bypass towns and cities, especially when, as in this case, one has reason to suspect that enemy forces may be pocketed therein. What happens is a wiley enemy lets you run on by and then darts out to attack your supply lines. Which is what the Iraqis now did.

On day four, a reporter embedded with the Third Division described what appeared to be flying columns of Iraqis dashing out of the city of Najaf.[30] These harassing elements were small, comprising no more than six or seven men, and interestingly—as had been observed in Umm Qasr—they were not in uniform. They were wearing either balaklava masks or *kafeiyahs,* and sweat suits. They were armed with AK-47s and rocket propelled grenade launchers, mounted on Toyota pickup trucks, with 50 calibre machine guns set up behind them. In this they resembled the infamous "technicals," who appeared in the fight between Chad and its North African neighbor, Libya; that is, commandos, taking orders from no higher authority but who rather operated on their own. Once the harassers shot up the Americans' columns, they would scurry back inside the towns, as if daring the Americans to follow.

At first, the American commanders dismissed these raiders as mere nuisances. General Franks was particularly caustic. "I don't think," he said, "it's appropriate for senior military people to respond to the sort of hype that [is being] described."[31] Nonetheless, given the situation they were in, the Americans were vulnerable to such harassment. Umm Qasr was not open for the free flow of supplies; the brigades of the Third Division had dashed so far ahead their lines were stretched thin; most crucially, fuel—which above all else the column must have—was not getting through.[32]

On top of everything else, there were sandstorms.[33] This meant visibility was cut to a minimum. In places, parts of the American northward moving column strayed off course—inevitable, since you could not see a car's length ahead of you. This occasioned breakdowns; the column had to regroup then start up again.

The column moved day and night. Ordinarily this would have given the Americans an advantage, since they were equipped with infrared goggles which enabled them to see in the dark. But not in a sandstorm—the goggles did not work.

In the meantime, the harassers kept nipping away, picking off strays, and, in general, complicating the picture.

It was reported that these raiders actually were *Fedayeen*—Saddam's Fedayeen; that is, youngsters who had taken an oath to die for the Iraqi president. I find this explanation hard to accept, for a number of reasons. There was such an outfit; however, it appeared back in 1991 when the Iraqis first fought the Americans, and it had not figured significantly in that earlier conflict; it soon disappeared from view. Moreover, as reported, the Fedayeen was supposed to be headed by Hussein's son, Uday. Uday was a rake and a ne'er-do-well. He could not possibly have headed an outfit such as this, which performed at this early stage most effectively against the Americans.

Consequently, I do not believe that the Americans knew whom the Fedayeen were. Indeed, later on Tenet revealed to Bob Woodward that he had not a clue about them.[34] It is likely the case that the Americans were temporizing: having encountered significant resistance (which they had not anticipated), they groped for an explanation and devised this one about fanatical youth. By implying fanaticism, the Americans stayed on message, so to speak. They were refusing to concede that anyone other than diehards would do any fighting.

In addition to the army brigades, another Marine unit was moving up along the Euphrates and its destination was Nasiriyah. Nasiriyah was important because, located on the river, there were bridges there. Using these as crossing places, the Americans could invade the east bank; this would position them to ascend the high escarpment north of the city and that would put them on the level plateau that stretched to Baghdad.[35]

It was at Nasiriyah that the Americans ran into their first full-scale engagement with the Iraqis. Sharp clashes were reported. This occasioned a press conference by Rumsfeld in which he appeared with Air Force General Richard Meyers, the chairman of the Joint Chiefs. The two were peppered with questions from reporters who wanted to know, *Why all of a sudden this resistance? Had not the Defense Department said there would not be any such, and that, if resistance did materialize, it would be soon over with?*

Rumsfeld, as he was prone to do when pressured, lost his cool.[36] He insisted that the harassing attacks were isolated incidents, and Meyers added, "They're onesies and twosies. We're not going to worry about onesies and twosies."[37]

Be that as it may, the Nasiriyah complication proved major. There were only so many stretches along the Euphrates where an army could cross. At any putative crossing point the river banks had to be able to support tanks and trucks; the elevation had to be sufficiently high so that materiel could be borne across the waters; and, of course, there had to be bridges that could bear the weight of all the equipment the Americans were moving. Nasiriyah fulfilled all these conditions and evidently the Iraqis had figured out that the Americans would seek to cross here because they converged on the spot like swarms of angry hornets.[38]

As had occurred with Umm Qasr, journalists embedded with the American units initially reported the bridges had been taken—reports which almost immediately were contradicted.[39] A *New York Times* reporter described fire fights in which paramilitaries would dash out of Nasiriyah on their little trucks, dismount, and blast away at the Americans, standing up to tanks with mere rocket propelled grenade launchers. "It was suicidal," one U.S. Army man told a reporter. "I don't see what could possibly be motivating these people."[40]

Such actions evidently dismayed the Americans, probably for the reason that such was not expected.[41] They had been led to believe, through their indoctrination before the war, that resistance would not occur. That this sort of thing should go on—suicidal attacks on heavily armored columns by lone individuals or small groups armed with nothing more formidable than AK-47s—this was quite beyond their comprehension, and they reacted by showing irritation.[42]

The temporary inability of the American column to move forward emboldened the alarmists (back in Washington)—those who had predicted a costly fight—to speak out more forcefully. This brought Rumsfeld back to the podium in the Pentagon's briefing room. He declared the original strategy was working; he said he would keep to it. It was not he but his field commanders who were set on this, he said.[43]

Whatever Rumsfeld may have said in public, in fact he was shamming. Even as he spoke, the strategy was in the process of changing. The mad-dash-to-Baghdad was being put on hold; the focus was now on Nasiriyah, where the Marines would be given time to settle with the paramilitaries.[44]

The Marines attempted to overcome the resisters and force their way into the city. Immediately they became involved in a series of fire fights along a broad boulevard that ran the length of the city. This, the Marines later dubbed Ambush Alley.

What happened next is of particular significance. In accounts of the Nasiriyah action (appearing after the war was over) Marines who had fought there revealed that, along with the so-called Fedayeen, *civilians were fighting:* women, children, old men, and so on.

> He had never shot live ammo at human beings before, and he never imagined that this was how he would have to do it. He could see the people he was shooting at. Some of them were only meters away from him. There were no soldiers or military vehicles to shoot at. Some were women and children....

Yelling he pointed to a crowd of people in a square on the left-hand side of the road. Most of them were scattering, but as they split they revealed an Iraqi dressed in black, firing from the hip with an AK-47. He saw Wentzel fire the M203 grenade launcher, which arced in the air and landed in the middle of the fleeing crowd. Pieces of rock, debris *and people* [my emphasis] flew into the air. . . .

He couldn't believe it. He swore that was a kid firing an AK-47 at him. Just as he got ready to fire back, the kid ducked into a doorway. "Fuck. I've got to fire at anything that might be a threat."[45]

What is conspicuous in this account (and what was replicated in others like it) is the absence of men in uniform. To be sure there were mysterious combatants (the man dressed in black who emerged from the crowd in the description just quoted), but along with individuals such as this there were *women, children, and oldsters* who were taking part. Why were the people fighting?

I have a theory about the Fedayeen. I do not believe that they were fanatical youth, at all. I believe they were regular fighters, and Republican Guardsmen, who had doffed their uniforms to don civilian dress so as to meld in with the crowd. If this is what was happening, it would explain why the people fought.[46] The army, as I said above, was predominantly Shia. The cities where the Americans were running into these fierce fire fights were all Shia. If the army, the Iraqi army, had elected to fight, then it is natural the people would fight alongside it because these were their loved ones: husbands, sons, relatives.

The fact of the Iraqi army men fighting in mufti is also explicable from another angle. In the first Iraq War the Iraqi High Command had elected to fight conventionally: using tanks and armored personnel carriers, it had sought to fight a war of maneuver, and the Americans had easily been able to defeat them in that.

Now, in this war, (I believe) the Command switched approaches. It fought *unconventionally;* that is, a war of urban guerrillas, carried on from *inside* the southern cities. The aim being to try to lure the Americans into the cities, where in the mazes of side streets, alleys, and cul-de-sacs the heavily armored American units would find themselves at a disadvantage. In this sense one could say that the Iraqis were trying to duplicate conditions of the Lebanese Civil War, where the Lebanese and Palestinians discomforted the armor-heavy Israeli units, tying them up in fire fights from inside the warren of Beirut.

In any event, the implications of this turnabout are profound. This certainly shows that the Americans' intelligence, which they had gotten from the expatriates, was wrong.[47] But over and above this, it says something about the nature of the Iraqi general staff. If, as I am surmising, this was a deliberate strategy the Iraqis were pursuing, then it represents a calculated move on the generals' part. The Fedayeen actions were not random occurrences carried out by fanatical youth; they were part of a worked out strategy; they were the Iraqis' preconceived plan.

That would indicate not only a certain expertise on the generals' part but also that the military had the "will" to victory. They were not fighting *en melee*, but determinedly, according to a plan.

Indeed, there is a name for this kind of strategy: it is called outside-in defense.[48]

All of the foregoing is speculation on my part. However, there is evidence that what I am suggesting is true. For example, a number of prisoners taken in this war (and there were not a great many[49]) turned out to be army men in civilian dress. The first reported instance of a suicide bombing involved an Iraqi non-com, who, dressed as a civilian, approached an American checkpoint and blew himself up.[50] And, finally, as the war progressed, the U.S. military reported more and more of the so-called Fedayeen actions showed a high degree of command and control, which definitely would indicate professional involvement.

However, the best evidence of what I am saying is this. American ground units had suffered from sandstorms. The same had affected the U.S. Air Force: it was compelled to cancel planned bombing runs. However, on March 30, the sandstorms abated. American airmen spotted masses of Iraqis moving south from Baghdad. They were travelling in small groups (in other words, not a formal troop movement), and they were driving trucks, many of them Toyota pickups; these were converging on the southern cities.[51]

That says to me that the defenses of the cities were being supplied from Baghdad. The Iraqi High Command was detailing off army men and sending them south dressed as civilians[52] to operate independently from inside the cities. In other words, the Command was seeking to dictate the terms of combat. Rather than waiting for the Americans to come to them in Baghdad, the Iraqis were taking the war to the enemy.

Tim Pritchard, from whose book I was quoting above, wrote an op-ed piece in the *New York Times* in which he expressed the view that the Americans had missed an opportunity when they failed to attach due weight to what had gone on in Nasiriyah.[53] The action there showed the Iraqis were not disaffected from their government, as the Americans had been led to believe. With the exception of the Kurds, they rather supported it. Had the Americans drawn the proper conclusion, they might not have been caught unawares in the occupation phase (Pritchard wrote), when resistance flared so soon after the victory was declared.

I think Pritchard's view is prescient, but I think he might have carried it further. What was being revealed here was a capability, on the Iraqis' part, to fight this kind of urban guerrilla war. Nothing in the Iraqis' background indicated any such competency. All of the wars the Iraqi army fought were of another kind: conventional. That the Iraqis should so easily segue over into this totally different kind of warfare says something: as an enemy they were formidable under any circumstances, as would soon be brought out when the next phase of the resistance developed, in the occupation.

Of course, the Iraqis' could not hope to win, the power that the Americans could bring to bear being so great. But, as we will shortly see, their strategy was not without effect, because of how it forced the Americans to react.

The air war changed. Up till this point the Americans had been pursuing what is called leadership targeting. That is where the air force concentrates on bombing the capital, Baghdad, because that is where the leaders are. In the process it hits command-and-control facilities—things like defense ministry buildings—on the assumption that, if it can prevent the leadership from communicating with frontline fighters, the resistance will collapse.[54]

Now the strategy had switched to so-called attrition bombing. This is where the target list is broadened.[55] The Americans still were focused on Baghdad, but instead of bombing selectively they had begun to bomb *wholesale*. They began hitting Iraqi Republican Guard units around Baghdad and inside the city. They also hit telephone exchanges and the like. The rationale for this was set forth by John Warden, a leading proponent of the air war. Warden, a retired air force colonel, said in an interview that it did not do to be too conservative. Whereas one would certainly try to limit civilian casualties (he said) over-reliance on such an approach curtailed the effectiveness of the bombing. One had to go after, what Warden called, other centers of gravity.[56]

In the lead up to the war there had been two centers of gravity considered by the Americans. One was the leadership, Hussein and the men around him; the other, the Republican Guard. The Guard had played a pivotal role in imposing defeat on the Islamic Republic in the Iran-Iraq War. It was considered the regime's mainstay and sure defense. Given that the Guard units were all stationed around Baghdad, the Americans had expected to confront them there in the decisive battle at the end of the war. It may be that they now determined that the Iraqis were using the Guard to reinforce the cities of the South, sending them piece meal, in small units, as I said, and therefore the Americans started bombing the Guard positions inside and around Baghdad. I do not know this for a fact, however; it is speculation.

About this time, a terrible incident occurred as missiles fired by the Americans fell on a market in Baghdad, killing 58 people.[57] The next day another neighborhood in Baghdad was hit, and 14 more Iraqis, all civilians, died. The Americans claimed that they did not know whether these strikes had been caused by stray U.S. missiles. However, a U.S. military spokesman opined that they might have been contrived by the Ba'thists. In other words, to throw blame on the Americans, the Ba'thists had deliberately planted bombs in the neighborhoods.[58]

Be this as it may, from here on in such incidents abounded, as more and more civilian neighborhoods were hit, and consequently more civilians were killed. Speaking about the type of bombs being used, a senior U.S. military officer declared the Americans were now dropping so-called HCD's.[59] An HCD is a bomb that causes high collatoral damage. These were not precision instruments; rather they were bombs which spread destruction over a wide area.

The war was turning ugly. And, as might have been expected, as civilian casualties mounted, anger developed—not just in the Arab world (which one would have expected), but also in Europe. Demonstrations broke out after scenes of the carnage were broadcast over *Aljazeera,* the Arab broadcasting company based in Qatar. *Aljazeera* had correspondents in Iraq who dependably gave an anti-American slant to events.

Shortly after this the Americans destroyed *Aljazeera's* broadcasting facilities in Baghdad.[60] Again, they claimed this was not deliberate (a claim which *Aljazeera* disputed).

Some commentators now began comparing Allied bombings of the Iraqi cities with Dresden, the affair in World War II where the Allies carpet bombed that German city (along with others), to break the Germans' morale. Rumsfeld reacted angrily to this claim. "Oh my goodness, no," he said. He insisted the American side was well aware that, in a war of this kind, it was not only important to win, but to win justly.[61]

Through all of this one fact emerges; that is that perceptions of what was going on in Iraq diverged. The American commanders at the front were seeing a war that did not conform to perceptions of the civilians in the Pentagon. This asymmetry of views came out sharply when, on March 28, Lieutenant General William Wallace, the V Corps commander, speaking from the theater, said, "This war was not the one we war-gamed for." Implied was that the Iraqis, whom the Americans had believed would be a pushover, were putting up a much stiffer fight than anticipated.[62]

Rumsfeld, according to *New York Times* correspondent Michael Gordon, hit the roof over this.[63] He ordered Franks to relieve Wallace of his command, and, according to Gordon, Lieutenant General David McKiernan, the allied land war commander, felt compelled to fly to Franks's headquarters in Qatar to plead for the general. (Wallace was allowed to keep his job.)

Here, one could say, was evidence of hubris—the hubris of the civilians in the Pentagon. Hubris is characterized by the inability to confront reality.[64] Those so afflicted cannot assimilate information that conflicts with their set views. In this instance, what the civilians could not see was that, for the Americans, the war was starting to spin out of control.

Rumsfeld was obviously in a bind. He had rushed the war by inserting troops into Iraq while an essential component of the force (the Fourth Division) was still en route. Now, when the Iraqis had managed to impede the Americans' advance, the secretary had to regain the initiative. The only way he could (since he had insufficient ground troops) was to use the Air Force. He escalated the bombing, broadening and deepening the target list, but this was not without serious adverse effect.

The Americans had committed the cardinal error of underestimating their enemy; now they were about to compound that mistake. They thought that by intensifying the bombings they could bring the Ba'thists to heel, but the Ba'thists were not about to capitulate, and that virtually committed the Americans to conducting more and more bombing raids, and that, in turn, increased the amount of infrastructure that would be destroyed. All of this was going to make problems for the Americans in the occupation phase.

Without meaning it, the Americans had made themselves hostage to the Ba'thists' will: the longer the Ba'thists held out, the more destruction the Americans would be forced to inflict—destruction which at all costs they ought to have been seeking to avoid.

In Basrah, a humanitarian crisis was developing. The British (as I said) had been operating on the assumption that Basrah was not a military objective. They shared the Americans' view that, because Basrah was a Shia community, its citizens would rise and deliver the city into Allied hands. When that did not happen, the British were temporarily at a loss. Subduing Basrah by force was not an option—at least not an inviting one, especially for British troops who had had experience of Northern Ireland. But neither was keeping up the siege a solution. Reports had begun coming out of the city of food shortages—but, more alarmingly, of water. Kofi Annan, the UN secretary general, addressed a plea to the British, to have a care for the civilian population.[65] The fact of the water being cut off raises the question, How did this happen? The British must have targeted the facilities, or else they had hit the electric grid, which would have shut the facilities down.

In any event, the British commander—perhaps in an attempt to temporize—claimed a revolt was just now getting under way.[66] This hope was dashed when UN personnel stationed across the Tigris (in Iran) reported they could not see any signs of unusual disturbances in the city.

Thus, it was that on March 30 the British, too, began lobbing bombs into heavily populated urban areas—initially they used artillery, later planes.[67] The British claimed that their targets were restricted to official buildings, but as Mohammad Saeed Sahhaf, Iraq's information minister, charged, "There are civilians inside those buildings!"[68]

As with the Americans, so, too, the British sought to deflect blame on to the Ba'thists. They said they were forced to bomb official sites because that is where the Iraqi fighters were lurking. It is noteworthy how the Allies consistently resorted to this defense. They took the attitude that what the Iraqis were doing—by fighting inside the cities—was not right (or, one might say, in the British case, cricket). Whereas the American and British targeting of cities with aerial attacks—this was okay. To be sure, in wartime each side seeks to defend its conduct. But what the Allies were discovering was that, as long as *Aljazeera* operated, they could not control the news. I said earlier that demonstrations were erupting in Europe, now they developed as well in Egypt and Jordan, two repressive regimes, as well as firm allies of the United States. That ordinarily suppressed populations would come out in support of Iraq was embarrassing, both to the Americans and to the leaders of these countries.

What the Americans (and the British) were being exposed to here was the tendency, natural in human beings, to take sides. As long as the Allies could dominate events, they could hope to squelch alternative perceptions. Indeed, had the war gone as planned—with the Allies scoring a quick, knockout victory—it is certain their narrative would have prevailed: the resistance would have been seen as a hopeless attempt by a ruthless regime to delay the inevitable. That is how history has portrayed the war in Afghanistan: no one (that I am aware) took the part of the Taliban. But the Afghan War was over practically before it commenced, with only slight casualties on the American side (and not nearly the losses among the Afghans the Iraqis suffered).

Earlier I suggested that the Iraqi military, by adopting civilian garb, might be seeking to confuse the enemy.[69] Reports now began coming out of "atrocities" (is how the American command portrayed them) of[70] incidents where "civilians" would approach checkpoints manned by Americans and, then, when within range, attack.[71] In other reported instances, Americans driving in convoy through Iraqi towns would find themselves suddenly under fire from seemingly innocent civilians lined up to watch them pass (in the accounts of Marines fighting inside Nasiriyah this tactic was frequently reported).[72]

This sort of maneuver has an unfortunate result: traumatized Americans elect to shoot first and ask questions later. An American colonel gave voice to this dilemma (of not being able to distinguish combatants from civilians): "We don't know who's the enemy anymore," he said.[73] This way civilians get killed, many of them shot by U.S. soldiers at checkpoints. All unintentional, to be sure, but nonetheless bound to cause resentment among Iraqis (which probably was what the Ba'thists were aiming for).

In one incident Americans were caught in an ambush as they drove past an Iraqi mosque. Having been warned to give such buildings a wide berth (lest they offend the sensibilities of the Muslims), the soldiers were surprised at being fired on by resisters set up inside the building. Hospitals, too, were used in this way.[74]

Thus it was that the Americans began taking casualties. Since reports from the field were censored it was impossible to know precisely the losses sustained. Through April 6, 2003, the *New York Times* reported 89 American fatalities in the war. This, Michael O'Hanlon, a military analyst at the Brookings Institution, saw as a low figure.[75] But for the Americans, who had expected to lose few, if any, of their own, even this many was a lot.

And, of course, the Iraqi casualties were higher, much higher. Here again it is impossible to state accurately what they were. The Americans claimed they were not keeping count of enemy losses. Still, an international antiwar consortium led by Marc Herold, a professor at the University of New Hampshire, estimated between 877 and 1,050 civilians, not including military casualties (this based on news reports).[76] And the World Health Organization (WHO) reported Baghdad hospitals were seeing 100 combat casualties per hour on April 8, the day the battle for control of the city was at its most intense.[77]

The war had now devolved into what one American officer graphically described as a "game of smash-mouth football."[78] Having given up hope of an early Ba'thist capitulation, the Americans were having to grind the enemy into submission.

On March 26 the Americans fought their way inside Nasiriyah. They then began moving across the Euphrates. Still the bridges were not secured, because the Iraqis continued to raid the column from inside the city. The Marines were compelled to widen the perimeter surrounding the bridges, so as to create a safe zone.

As this was going on, additional fierce fire fights developed in Najaf and Samawah. Najaf was particular trouble because here is where the shrine of the Shias' patron saint, Ali, is located.[79] The resisters actually edged as close to the shrine as possible, practically inviting the Americans to shell their positions, with the hope, obviously, that they would damage the shrine, which would have further enraged the faithful.

The holdup at Nasiriyah was overcome, as the Marines were eventually able to push the Iraqis back so the column could cross the river. The Americans now commenced to roll across the dead flat plateau to the capital where the Republican Guards—or what was left of those units, so thoroughly bombed were they—awaited them.[80]

According to their original plan, the Americans intended to throw a ring around the capital. This would enable them to starve the besieged into submission—if they so chose—and also they meant to prevent the Republican Guard divisions stationed north of Baghdad from getting inside Baghdad. This matter of the Republican Guards north of Baghdad seeking to enter, I think, is worth commenting on.

There were two Republican Guard divisions in the North, supposedly there to defend against a push from that quarter by the Americans. To be sure, no substantial second front ever developed in the largely Kurdish provinces of the North because of Ankara's refusal to allow the Americans to use Turkish territory as a staging area. However, American Special Operations units had parachuted into the Kurdish area where they were welcomed by the Kurds, who almost uniformly had lined up on the American side.

Now, however, the Ba'thists evidently decided that, since there was not a significant threat likely to develop in the northern sector, this freed the Guard divisions to enter Baghdad (for the last-stand defense).[81] It is possible (as some reporters commented) that the Guards, in entering Baghdad were seeking to lose themselves in the city; in effect, take French leave. However, subsequent reports cast doubt on this.

I said that one of the options relative to taking Baghdad which the Americans were entertaining was to starve the besieged into surrender; in other words, not go into the city in force; not subject themselves to house-to-house fighting. However given what was happening in Basrah, this was becoming less of an attractive proposition. There were mounting reports of real suffering in the southern city, suffering which the British could not allay because the resisters refused to surrender and the Basrawis—for whatever reason—refused to revolt.

Moreover, Iraqi official state television beamed reports of Hussein going about Baghdad, pressing the flesh, as we say.[82] Crowds gathered around him, seemingly warmly receptive. The *New York Times* cast doubt on the authenticity of these receptions, saying they might have been staged. Still, such scenes did not facilitate the Allies' psyche war operations: the Americans were trying to break the Iraqis' morale; the last thing they wanted was for Baghdad to turn into another Stalingrad.[83]

Shortly after this, American air raiders hit the official television station in Baghdad, putting it temporarily off the air; however, it soon came back.[84]

What, in fact, was the situation inside the capital at this its last hour? Obviously there was a great deal of devastation as the bombed-out areas multiplied daily. The Americans were using lethal ordinance: 2,000- to 5,000-pound bunker-busting bombs, cruise missiles, and so on. At the same time they insisted they were not carpet bombing, although there are conflicting reports on this: it appeared they might be doing so against the Guards units. The Americans initially had tried to attack the Guards using Apache helicopters, but in one fierce engagement 33 of the airships were driven off and at least one chopper was shot down by Iraqi ground fire.[85] After that it was reported B-52s were being deployed against the Guardsmen, striking from high altitudes—the procedure adopted when carpet bombing.[86]

In any event, any one of these huge bombs landing in a neighborhood would likely cause terrible destruction. The western press corps inside the city reported none of this; the *New York Times* and *Washington Post* reporters concentrated on filing mood pieces. One such story, by a *Washington Post* reporter, painted an eerie picture.[87] The dust storms raged. Anyone who has ever experienced one of these knows how unsettling they can be: they cast a reddish pall over everything; their constant blowing gets on one's nerves; there is not a possibility of relief, and, of course, one cannot go about out-of-doors while they are blowing—not with the dust choking one's nostrils, cutting off breathing.

So the city appeared in many quarters to be deserted, and yet regularly double decker red public transportation buses made the rounds. With no one to service, they nevertheless trawled the neighborhoods. In some areas markets kept operating; newsboys hawked the daily paper. A *New York Times* reporter attempted to talk to people, but they dismissed him, turning his queries aside brusquely. Officials to whom the reporter spoke, appeared (he said) "to be trying to convey a façade of normality." This, the reporter construed as "redolent of an authoritarian elite in deep denial, incapable of grasping reality, either about their external enemies or the mood of less powerful Iraqis, because of years of listening mainly to echoes of themselves."[88]

I think this matter of the officials (and of the ordinary Iraqis) evincing calm in the face of crisis is noteworthy; however, I think the reporter misses the significance of what he was witnessing. As in the first Iraq War, the devastation wrought by the aerial bombing was horrendous. That Iraqi morale could hold up *for three weeks* under this kind of pounding was extraordinary. The Iraqis had no air force (they literally did not have one—it was not a case of the Americans having destroyed it; *from the first it did not exist*). There was not much that they could do, therefore, but hunker down and absorb the blows. What enabled the Iraqis to hold out, I think, was party discipline. Iraq, under the Ba'th, was a controlled society, and the agent of control was the central state apparatus. As long as that held up, things could get on. As long as officials went about performing assigned tasks; as long as they kept up appearances, the mood of the population remained calm. But, as soon as the officials cracked everything fell apart; the edifice of control disintegrated.

The Americans had originally expected Hussein and the top Ba'thists would try to, as we say, cop a plea: they would seek a deal, allowing them to go into exile. It therefore surprised the Americans when the Ba'thists held on in the capital, standing up to the deadly air attacks. Now the Americans revised their view: they decided the leadership would die in the capital: like Hitler, Hussein would perish in his underground bunker. A romantic idea, but not very realistic. It appears that what the Ba'thists were aiming for was to drag the battle out in the hope that international pressure would force a halt before total defeat was imposed.[89]

If that was the strategy, it was a hopeless one. Whom, after all, were the Ba'thists counting on to come to their aid? *Not their Arab brothers, certainly.* Leaders like Mubarak (of Egypt) and Abdullah (of Saudi Arabia) were keeping resolutely clear of helping out the Ba'thists. Indeed on April 2, Saudi Arabia's Foreign Minister Prince Saud al Faisal called on Saddam Hussein to surrender himself and go into exile, thus sparing the Iraqis more punishment. To which, Taha Yasin Ramadan, Iraq's vice president, responded, "You failure, go to hell! You are too small to talk to the leader of Iraq, and those who will be swept away from the land of the Arab world are people like you. You are a minion and a lackey!"[90]

What about the United Nations? The United Nations was in no position to provide succor. With the Security Council dominating every aspect of its performance, the United States (and Britain) easily could balk ameliorative action the United Nations might wish to take.

The Russians? The Chinese? *The Europeans? There was no one.* The Iraqis were doomed. It was just a matter of time before they would be forced to capitulate.

In the South, the British had begun making progress. On March 30, a commando unit succeeded in penetrating to the heart of Basrah, where it blew up two statues of Hussein[91] in an attempt to provoke a reaction among the Basrawis—the British were still hoping for a revolt. Still, nothing materialized.

Then, on April 9, perhaps tired of waiting, the British made the first of a series of penetrations in force into Basrah. And the public response was surprising. Instead of being welcomed joyously, the British practically were ignored. Indeed they were forced to look on helplessly *as the Basrawis indulged in an orgy of looting.*[92]

Basrah was now down; Umm Qasr was down; only Baghdad and some provincial cities were still left standing. As for Baghdad, the Americans were yet debating how to handle it: whether to fight their way in or not.

In discussions with American military men, held subsequent to the take-over, I have noted that practically all interpret the U.S. Army's next move as inspired. I am talking about the Thunder Run. On April 6, the Americans sent a column of M1 tanks and M2 Bradley fighting vehicles speeding through Baghdad. They entered from the southern outskirts of the city and roared north, then west on the airport expressway.[93] This, the American military seems to have convinced itself, is what ended the war. That run, in which the column shot up everything that moved, the Americans evidently believe is what triggered the ultimate collapse. This, the Americans say, "sent a message" to the Iraqis that the war was over.

But the Thunder Run, however sensational it may have been, did not cause the fighting to cease. The resistance carried on for several days afterward. Fierce fights took place inside Hussein's presidential compound two days after the Thunder Run occurred.[94] This engagement continued all of one night, and with the dawn a few ragged defenders still were found blasting away. "I don't see what motivates these guys," one American officer wondered aloud. "Saddam could be popped tomorrow and still they'd fight."[95]

The *Washington Post* now reported that Iraqi tribesmen had begun arriving in the city, to assist in the final defense. The tribesmen raised their red standards on improvised barricades.[96] There was also, to be sure, defeatism: one of the Shia divines, Ayatollah Ali Sistani, (about whom I will have more to say in the fourth chapter) issued a religious ruling to the faithful not to resist the Allied forces.[97]

There was also a fierce defense at the Republican Guard headquarters, sited on an eminence from which beleaguered Guardsmen attempted to hold out. An American serviceman described the fight as "scary." When the Americans finally fought there way inside the compound, it was "awful" he said, "stinking, bloated corpses. ..."[98]

This fact of the Guards having, in a manner of speaking, gone down with the ship is, I think, significant. The Americans insisted, after the war had ended, that the Guard had "melted away"; at the end it simply disappeared without attempting to put up a fight.[99]

However, if one consults the clips, this was not the case. The Guard stood up to the carpet bombing outside of Baghdad, then when the bombing became too intense it withdrew inside the capital, and finally it put up a defense of its headquarters.[100]

I think the Americans' focus on the Guard, and their claims that it did not fight, is a red herring. I think it is an attempt by the Americans to explain the abrupt cessation of hostilities, because the manner in which the war ended does not reflect well on the American conduct of the war.

Iraq was blasted. The bombing which had gone on for almost three weeks escalated to such an extent some neighborhoods were virtually obliterated, so battered were they.

To be sure, I do not think the Americans ever meant for this to happen; that is that they should cause such awful destruction; however, they were driven to it. Since the Iraqis kept fighting, the only way of getting the war over with was to bomb—to put it cruelly, blow them away.

In the process of doing that the Americans caused considerably more destruction than they ever intended.

In any event, once the Ba'thists had absorbed all the punishment they could take, I think, they gambled on one last throw of the dice. They attempted to make a final stand, and in line with that they committed all their available forces to defend the perimeter rim of the city. That left the streets of Baghdad unpoliced, and forthwith the Iraqis fell on the contents of the bombed out office buildings, to commence an orgy of looting.

According to reports, the looting that went on was horrendous. Iraqis invaded private residences, seizing whatever they could haul away. What they could not scoop up—because it was bolted down—they tore loose from its moorings.

Once the looting commenced, anarchy reigned.

I think it was the combination of all these things that brought the abrupt termination of the war.

In that respect, I think we need to reassess the air war strategy. Rumsfeld had been insisting throughout the war that it was humane; that with the use of precision guided bombs and missiles, this type of war was more humane than any ever waged.

I do not agree. The air war strategy makes provision for escalation, and once one escalates, the target list expands. Soon targets are being hit which ought never to have been selected. For example, at the end of the war water in Baghad was shut off—that could only have come about if the Americans hit the electric grid.[101]

So I would say, then, if this war showed anything it was the inefficacy of the air war.

But, you say, What about the result? It may have been unethical, but it certainly was effective. The Iraqis were forced to submit; the war was over in three weeks!

But what was the condition of Iraq at the end? It was blasted, and, as I said above, the infrastructure which the Americans were going to have to depend on to run the country was practically gone.

Moreover since Rumsfeld had not sent enough troops into the country, the Americans could not prevent the looting once it started. So whatever infrastructure was left after the bombing was stripped bare by the looters.

In other words the war was not the unalloyed triumph Bush made it out to be. Subsequently the president claimed the Iraqis did not fight. Those who did, he said, were "forced" to do so.[102] Anyone who did not fight, according to Bush, was "murdered by the republic Guard" [sic].[103]

All nonsense. The fact, however, that the Americans would practice this pretense is important in light of what developed next; that is the eruption of resistance in the occupation phase.

As Pritchard said, the Americans were forewarned. There was ample evidence that conditions inside Iraq were not as the Americans had anticipated. Not one Iraqi army unit surrendered without a fight. There were no uprisings in any of the Shia cities to oust the Ba'th. None of the top Ba'thists fled the country, including and most notably Saddam Hussein. In other words, the degree of solidarity was exceptional. But most surprising the people fought alongside the army. As I said above this was explicable from the fact that the army was largely Shia and, in all the southern cities fought over, Shias predominated. It was natural for the people to support their troops under those circumstances.

But what this said to the Americans, and what they ought to have picked up on but did not, was that the Iraqis were not disposed to accept the occupation. In the next chapter we will see how the resistance revived, and what caused it to do so. In line with that we are going to be looking at some background on the army, because, I think, the officers of Hussein's army started the resistance. So we need to know something about what the army, as an institution, was like.

2

The Iraqi Army

My explanation of why the United States went to war with Iraq is simple: when empires break apart those entities formerly associated with them become vulnerable. In the eyes of certain powerful parties in the United States, Iraq was a satellite of the Soviet empire and consequently it seemed right to them that America should acquire it.[1] The mystery is, why have the Americans not been able to bring it off, and the answer that I am going to suggest is that they were thwarted by the appearance of a formidable resistance inside the country. The object of the study now will be to develop how that resistance came into being. I think it was incited by ex-officers of the Iraqi army. One of the core beliefs of western intelligence about the Iraqi army was that it was totally under the thumb of the civilian Ba'thists. What I am going to show in this chapter is that that condition changed over the course of the Iran-Iraq War, until the army became a practically autonomous institution. Then in the third chapter I will show how that changed condition affected the Americans when they set up their occupation over Iraq.

American intelligence, in my experience, misapprehended the quality of the Iraqi army: it underestimated the officers' competency and their *esprit de corps*. This created conditions for a major intelligence failure which developed soon after the occupation was established. The Americans *dissed* the Iraqi officers and then when the officers bridled they ignored their complaints, thus making a bad situation worse. This confrontation led to what now gives every appearance of turning into a widespread national revolt.

On the assumption that the reader lacks familiarity with the army, and with its standing as a fighting force, I will use this chapter to describe its professional growth. The matter of its being professional is important because otherwise it would be hard to explain how the revolt got going. It is not usual for an army, that only just has been defeated, to within days turn around and reconstitute itself as an underground with which to begin the war anew. Which essentially is what the Iraqi army did.

For the purposes of this study the Iraqi army has no history worth noting going back farther than the 1930s. The British, who took over the mandate for Iraq in the 1920s, refused to allow Iraq's first king, Faisal, to impose conscription, which would have produced a bona fide military arm of the government.[2] The army that existed (under the British) was largely ceremonial. This makes sense since the king was to all intents a puppet of the British, and they clearly felt that he would be more manageable without a genuine fighting force.[3] However, the League of Nations granted Iraq independence in 1932 and Faisal forthwith established an army separate from British control.[4]

He no sooner did so than a significant flap developed over his creation. This was an incident of a kind that would repeat throughout the history of modern Iraq (and most conspicuously in the present day in the controversy over Iraq's alleged genocidal campaign against the Kurds). The incident that I am about to relate was initially construed to be a great human rights tragedy. The army of Faisal is supposed to have massacred elements of Iraq's Assyrian population. "Massacre" is British diplomat Gerald De Gaury's description. De Gaury was an advisor to the first king, Faisal. According to him:

> In 1933, while Faisal was in Europe, three hundred Assyrians were massacred by troops commanded by General Bakr Sidqi in the village of Simel in the Mosul province of northern Iraq. Whoever fired the first shot in a brush on the Syrian frontier...there could be no justification for the shooting down by the Iraqi army of numbers of Assyrians in villages far away....[A]n even worse massacre was planned by the Iraqi army to take place at Alqush. The people killed were entirely innocent. It was enough for them to be Assyrians to be shot. The [Assyrians] in Dohuk were taken away in batches of eight or ten for a short distance from the villages in lorries and there turned out and machine-gunned.[5]

De Gaury particularly was outraged that Sidqi was acclaimed by the Iraqis as a hero—and what was worse (he says), that he later was decorated and promoted by the Iraqi government. De Gaury, however, gives a spin to his account; looked at from another angle the affair is not so clear cut. The Assyrians were *introduced* into Iraq after World War I; they had not been resident there, having previously been domiciled out-of-country. The British brought them to Iraq to serve in a levy, as they called it. This was a constabulary force, its duty being to guard British military installations, and in the process of doing so friction developed between the Assyrians and the native Iraqis.[6] Undoubtedly some of this friction could be attributed to different religions: Iraq, of course, was primarily—overwhelmingly—Muslim;

the Assyrians were Christian. However, to make the affair out to be an ethnic quarrel, that is, Arabs against non-Arab Assyrians, cannot be maintained. Sidqi was a Kurd.

The incident De Gaury relates occurred after the 300 who were killed had decamped from Iraq to Syria. The British—as the mandate drew to a close—ended certain engagements, among them their special relationship with the Assyrians. The new government of Faisal offered them land grants and because the 300 involved in the incident did not deem the grants sufficient they quit the country (in a pet, evidently). The French, who held the Syrian mandate, turned them back at the border, and in returning to Iraq the Assyrians ran into the Iraqi army unit under Sidqi. Shots were exchanged, and, as De Gaury says, it is not known who fired first.[7]

Viewed this way, the affair becomes a matter of sovereignty. The new government of Faisal would naturally want to control its borders; it would also want all communities resident therein to be beholden to it. The 300 Assyrians were presuming to exit and return by no one's leave but their own, something which could be seen as unacceptable. So then the affair was not a matter of premeditated human rights violations but a case where a newly sovereign government seeks to assert its authority, and has, in the process of so doing, to challenge what till then had been a virtually autonomous community in its midst.

As I said, the affair resonates today because, in so many particulars, it mirrors the claim of the Kurds to have been subjected to a genocidal campaign by the Ba'thists. And like the present day case it raises important questions, such as when is violence gratuitous, and even vicious, and when is it a part of the state's prerogative to enforce its writ over its territory? Or put another way, when is violence perhaps mandated because otherwise the state cannot function?

The Iraqi army's next significant showing on the world scene comes during World War II when it rebels, seeking to establish ties to the Axis. The revolt was crushed by the British, who landed troops from the Indian subcontinent, after which Iraq was effectively occupied by them for the duration of the war. For the Iraqi army to have rebelled against the British—in wartime—was extraordinary. Discounting rebellious activity in Ireland, as far as I am aware, this is the only instance of a colony of the British (which effectively is what Iraq was) seeking to break away by going over to the side of the Axis.

The events leading up to the revolt developed in 1940, and stretched into 1941. For a time, the Iraqi army besieged the British air base at Habaniyah, but was unable to take it.[8] There was some aid forthcoming from the Germans, but nothing of significance (at the time of the coup, the Germans had their hands full preparing to attack the Soviet Union). Had the affair been better managed, it might have seriously compromised the Allied war effort. The leading actors of the coup either fled the country, or in a few cases paid with their lives. Those executed subsequently were accounted martyrs by nationalist-minded Iraqis.

After World War II, it became obvious that Britain's career of empire was over. It fell prey to the treatment I just described, of a failing empire facing dismemberment by its erstwhile rivals. However, in the case of the British they had developed a fail-safe option: they sought to enlist the Americans in the management of their Middle East holdings, creating a kind of Anglo-Saxon condominium. In respect to Iraq and the Persian Gulf, the British proposed to formalize a pact with the Americans, which would include the countries of the so-called northern tier: Turkey, Iran, Pakistan, and Iraq. This arrangement, known as the Baghdad Pact, was ostensibly set up to guard against putative Soviet moves into the Gulf (but of course it also safeguarded Britain's overseas oil empire).[9] America was to supply the muscle and act as paymaster in chief; Britain, with its long history of area involvement, would provide the administrative support.[10]

The plan never really worked. The Americans, for reasons that are open to speculation, held back from becoming a full member of the new treaty organization, although they "associated" with it. In the eyes of the locals, this stance doomed the pact: the Shah of Iran, for example, did not think the pact amounted to much after America failed to assume full membership.

That was 1955. In 1958, the Iraqi army once more revolted, this time successfully ousting the Hashemites. In the process of so doing, the army triggered a popular upheaval so ferocious that, among Middle East observers, it is still looked back on with awe. An Iraqi army unit assassinated the king, the queen, the crown prince, his sister, and a number of royal retainers, after they had corralled them in the palace yard. The really awful (in some instances stomach-turning) deeds, however, were perpetrated in the streets of Baghdad by the mob.

Says De Guary: "the Crown Prince's body—the hands and feet cut off—was dragged through the streets, tied up naked for exhibition and run over by cars, until finally, after souvenir hunters had had their way, there remained only a piece of backbone and its flesh to throw aside."[11]

Here we have another graphic word-picture (similar to that of the Assyrians), bringing to mind yet another image of the American security workers ambushed in Fallujah (in April 2004), killed, and their corpses strung aloft on a railway bridge. The horror of that image was the glee with which the Iraqis cavorted around the dangling corpses.

Brigadier General Abdul Karim Qasem, who led the 1958 coup and who became the first republican ruler of Iraq, was after this regarded with extreme distaste by the erstwhile British masters of Iraq. They also deprecated him for his social origins: Qasem was, along with many other officers who made the coup, lower class; in fact he was a scholarship boy in the first class of the newly created (under Faisal) Iraqi military academy.[12]

Qasem was presumed to be amenable to leading his country into union with Colonel Gamel Abdul Nasser's Egypt. This was the 1950s, a period of intense ferment in the Middle East, largely due to Nasser's takeover in Egypt and his subsequent championing of Arab nationalism. Nasser and the Egyptian Free Officers fomented their revolt against Egypt's King Farouk in 1950 (a takeover much more pacific than that of the Iraqis).[13] Now, thanks to the Egyptians' inspired propagandizing, the colonel presided over an informal empire of Arabs, knit by ideology.

Arab nationalism was built around the idea that the Arabs are one people. Thus the existing national divisions (in Arab lands) are presumed to be artificial. If the Arabs were to take their place of prominence on the world scene (according to Nasser), they must unify. The idea seduced a lot of people in the Middle East; whether it was ever a realistic proposition is debatable; it certainly gave the Egyptians leverage, enabling Nasser to pose as a leader of the so-called Non-Aligned Movement along with Tito of Yugoslavia and Nehru of India. It did something else, however, something specific to the Middle East: it set Egypt up to pressure rich Arabs. The rulers of the Gulf states, advantaged by having all that oil, were led to understand (by Nasser) that this wealth belonged to the Arabs, generally.

It was perhaps for this reason—that is, because Iraq had oil which Qasem did not want to share—that he fought shy of entering the Egyptian embrace. However, his refusal did not sit well with other officers who made the coup with him. The general was continually being importuned by them to, in a manner of speaking, get with it. To resist being stampeded into a move he felt was wrong (wrong for Iraq and wrong for him), Qasem sought alliances elsewhere, notably with the Communists.

Americans do not generally think of Iraq—a country in the Persian Gulf—as part of the Russian sphere of influence. But throughout the nineteenth century and into the twentieth, the Czarist empire was continually pressing south, intruding into Iran and Turkey (two countries bordering Iraq). I said above that the Assyrians were a refugee people, brought to Iraq by the British. They originally were living in what is now northern Turkey, and when World War I broke out they took the side of the Allies against the Ottoman Empire.[14] They did so after having been propositioned by the Russians, who promised Cossack regiments to assist them in revolt. As had occurred with the Iraqis and the Germans, promised aid never materialized, and this forced the Assyrians to flee their ancestral home when the Ottomans descended on them in a punitive expedition.

In the same way that the Czar propagandized the Assyrians, the Czar's successors, the Bolsheviks, sought to cultivate Iraqis in World War II. As a country allied with the Americans and British in that war, the Soviet Union was enabled to open an information office in Baghdad while the war was going on, whence it reached out, primarily to the Iraqi underclass, mobilizing adherents in the cause of international communism. According to

Hannah Batatu, by the time World War II had ended, the Communist Party of Iraq was the most powerful such party in the Middle East.[15]

This was really something. One of the distinguishing characteristics of Arabs was that they almost never succumbed to the appeal of Marxism. But, according to Batatu, this was not the case with the Iraqis, who turned on to it in large numbers. This proved both a torment and a boon to Qasem. Although he had constantly to watch out, lest the Communists become too strong, he yet was motivated to wield them as a foil against the Arab nationalists: in the face of pressures emanating from the pro-Nasserist faction, he would open up to the Communists and vice versa.

For the years that Qasem remained in power he continually juggled alliances, and this constant back-and-forth made for extreme volatility. More than once the Sole Leader (as he called himself) found that he was unable to keep control, as various factions in Iraq battled each other. This was not a case of their contending at the ballot box (to be sure there never was such a thing as free elections). Rather this a was a species of direct action, two serious outbreaks of which occurred—the first in Mosul in March 1959, the second in Kirkuk four months later.[16]

Events surrounding these disturbances are complex, so much so that they are almost impossible to reconstruct. So many elements came into play, determining causality is a matter of judgment. For example, *class* very much was involved. Part of what drove the actions (in both instances) was the land reform policy of Qasem, a policy he sought to enact over the objections of not only Iraq's Arab landholders but also, as we will see in chapter three, Kurdish aghas, too, resented attempts to expropriate their holdings.

In the first action, in Mosul, powerful Arab landlords had, according to Batatu, begun to plot against Qasem. Communist supporters of the president, getting wind of this, informed him of it, and then, in collusion with Qasem, they maneuvered to force the plotters into tipping their hand. They arranged to hold a Peace Partisans rally in the city, summoning their followers from all over the country to participate. According to Batatu, the government obliged by providing free rail travel to the leftists.[17]

Many of the adherents were of the underclass, but not all were Arabs; there were numerous poor Kurds who also attended,[18] and this changed the character of the rally—communal rivalries boiled over as Kurds fought Arabs; Turkomans fought Kurds. And there was yet another division, for among those who had plotted with the landowners were Arab nationalist officers; in other words, Nasserists against Communists. That is why I say that it is almost impossible to figure out what was at the root of these disturbances.

In any event, the atrocities committed in the flare-ups were horrific. People were buried alive, strung up from lamp posts, dragged from ropes on the backs of cars, and so on.[19]

Among the army officers who took part as adherents of the Arab national-ist cause were so-called Ba'thists, a right wing party whose name in Arabic means revival. What we see here is a breakdown within the country of forces on the left, allied to Qasem, and those on the right, among which the Ba'thists may be said to have occupied the vanguard position.

Qasem came out on top in these twin contests, but the strain that the riots put on the system severely weakened not just it but Qasem's hold over the country as well.

Overwhelmed by the ferocity of the outbreaks, Qasem, with reason, could have been expected to abandon his loner status and sought entry into one of the two camps, that of the Soviet Union or the West. Qasem had no regard for the Russians, and he hated the British. As for the Americans, he had alienated them with his plans for Iraq's oil industry: early in his regime he espoused takeover, and in 1961 followed through by declaring all but a relatively small portion of Iraq's fields nationalized. He also, that year, presided over the founding of the Organization of Petroleum Exporting Countries (OPEC).[20] The American and British oil companies (Exxon, Mobil, BP, and Royal Dutch/Shell) had been active in Iraq [through the Iraq Petrolem Company (IPC)] since the 1920s. Naturally they wanted nothing to do with the Sole Leader, who expropriated what they regarded as their property.[21]

With so many inimical forces sniping away at him, Qasem finally (in 1963) was overthrown himself. He met the fate of the Hashemites: Ba'thist officers succeeded in fomenting a revolt, which culminated in Qasem's being gunned down outside his Defense Ministry, the equivalent of his palace.[22] (There is a particularly grisly photo of Qasem's crumpled body hunched against a courtyard wall.)[23]

Qasem's violent demise added to the myth of the Iraqis' innate vicious-ness. I think, however, it is wise to go slow with judgments of this sort: it never does to attribute actions of a whole people to psychological causes. The fact is that, during all of the years of the British occupation, economic conditions in Iraq were dreadful, and now, with the country in ferment, formerly repressed elements were breaking out. Given how long they had been kept down, it is no wonder the explosion was violent.

There is anecdotal evidence that the Ba'thists, in carrying out their coup, worked with the CIA.[24] They are supposed to have been supplied with lists of Communists to be proscribed, and, using the lists, they further are supposed to have systematically rounded up suspects and executed them. Casualties were extensive, well up in the thousands.[25] To world onlookers, the Iraqis were at it again. It did certainly appear that, under the republican form of rule, regime transfer in Iraq could not be carried out except by violence.

I will defer more extensive treatment of the Ba'th and focus here on one aspect of the party's rule. It is with the Ba'th that we note the appearance of the militia phenomenon, something which after this becomes a feature of Iraqi politics.

Qasem inherited, as I indicated above, a dangerous situation in that masses of urban poor, having been politicized—mainly by the Communists—were on tap, so to speak, for violent street actions. These people, restless, avid to assert themselves, and thus available for any kind of activity, could not simply be wished away. Once mobilized (during World War II), they became a persistent force in Iraq's political life.

Qasem's strategy for dealing with popular effervescence was to allow his adherents—mainly the Communists—to arm themselves. He is supposed to have let them requisition weapons for rallies, training camp sessions and the like, but otherwise the arms were kept under lock and key. That way, Qasem was able to keep a semblance of control.

The 1963 coup of the Ba'th was as much a civilian as a military action. Tanks invaded the capital; the air force assaulted the ministries with repeated bombing runs. But, still, had it not been for the participation of armed civilians the revolt would probably not have come off.[26] And, as a consequence of this, once the takeover was accomplished, the new rulers found they had to accommodate the civilian combatants.

As was the case with Qasem, the Ba'thists had to devise a means of neutralizing this unruly element.[27] The way they adopted was to institutionalize the violence by creating a paramilitary group, the so-called Popular Army (or National Guard, as some called it). This was an outfit whose members circulated, mainly in the capital, carrying out, as they called them, patrols, which they conducted under arms. Their specialty was harassing people on the street, stopping them to demand identification, and in some cases performing arrests.[28]

Unfortunately for them, the Popular Army men made no distinction for professional army officers. The Ba'th had come to power through a coup which could not have succeeded had there not been officers who, if they were not wholeheartedly sympathetic, at least had been willing to go along; some of these (although not members of the Ba'th) had delivered their units to the fight.

When the officers, who naturally were jealous of their status, found themselves being dressed down in public by individuals whom they viewed as hoodlums—they took umbrage. They served notice on their Ba'thist colleagues (among the military) that the militia had to go, and as a consequence, the Ba'thist officers turned on the civilian element of the party. They packed the militiamen's leader, Ali Saleh as Sa'di, off to exile in Spain.[29]

This triggered another violent eruption, a battle between the professional army units and Popular Army men which raged for an entire week. In the end, the militia was suppressed—or, at least tamped down for a time.

Manifest here is antagonism between popular (i.e., civilian) forces and the military. I do not know of any other instance in the Middle East where civilians were able to outmaneuver the military after a takeover like this. Coups of the sort that Qasem and his fellow officers effected are nothing unusual in this part of the world, but it usually is the case that the military quickly asserts control. Not so in Iraq.

I referred above to the militiamen as hoodlums. This was another peculiarity of the Ba'th. Like the Communists, the Ba'thists recruited from the underclass. These popular adherents tended to be young, and although many—as was the case with the Ba'th's most famous son, Saddam Hussein—attended university, few obtained degrees. Batatu points out that many of the original Ba'thists (again this was the case with Hussein) gravitated to Baghdad from the countryside (the *balad*), seeking work. Often they were destitute.

Not a few of the youths tried to enlist in the traditional liberal-style parties (Batatu cites the *Istiqlal,* or Constitution Party), only to find themselves rejected. Being poor and with not much hope of advancement careerwise, they were made aware the traditional parties were not interested in them. On the other hand, the Communist and Ba'thist parties, being revolutionary—insofar as they sought to take power through violent means (which certainly was something that the youth understood)—were more receptive. Young men like Sa'di and Hussein became immersed in the world of underground politics and like fish in water many swam to the top.

Thus we can say that the Ba'th constituted a unique phenomenon: although on the surface a traditional Arab nationalist party, dominated by army men, it yet had this civilian component, which, for reasons never fully explicated, it refused (or was unable) to repudiate. Since the civilians tended mainly to be youths, the movement also had a generational aspect. Interestingly, we encounter this same phenomenon when Ayatollah Ruhollah Khomeini takes power in Iran in the late 1970s when the Shah was overthrown.

Can one say then that the Iraqi Ba'th and the Iranian Islamic Republican parties were of a type? They were and they were not. In respect to the fact of both mobilizing out-of-work youth, yes, they definitely were similar. However, there were also differences, the most striking being that the Ba'th was resolutely secular; the Islamic Republican Party was of course religious. But also the Islamic Republicans came to power by *overcoming* the Shah's army, and later they purged the officers root-and-branch; the civilians in the Ba'th performed otherwise. In Iraq, the civilians occupied a subordinate role and worked with the officers, although (as we will see) they were on the lookout, waiting for a chance to maneuver the officers out of power.[30]

The new government which took over in Iraq (in 1963), once the civilian Ba'thists were curbed, was ideologically Arab nationalist and dominated by officers.[31] And there was not one of whom was not keen to ally with Egypt. The individual who led the coup was a non-Ba'thist colonel, Abdul Salam Aref. Aref was not a great leader. In fact, he was something of a blowhard:

a stump speaker, good at haranguing crowds. Despite his inadequacies, his reign stands in contrast to that which preceded it insofar as Iraq was reasonably peaceful. We have to put this down to the civilian element having been repressed.

Repressed but not entirely done away with, because throughout his regime, Aref—as had been the case with Qasem—sought to manipulate the rowdies. He had recourse to staged rallies, one of which I was able to experience personally. In 1963, I was sent by the *Milwaukee Journal* to cover the rebellion of the Barzani Kurds in northern Iraq. I had myself smuggled into the Kurdish area, intending to interview the old chief Mulla Mustafa Barzani. After leaving his encampment (through Iran) I made the mistake—in my naivete—of trying to reenter Iraq, legally, to interview Aref. Fortunately for me, I was intercepted, once in Baghdad, by the U.S. Embassy and hastily put under wraps as arrangements were made to fly me secretly out of the country. I spent one whole afternoon in the shuttered offices of the Iraqi Airlines. Outside in the street the government was holding a huge rally, with truckloads of peasants brought into the city, chanting and carrying on. Peering at the demonstration through the slats of the closed blinds, I was appalled at the brutality of the spectacle.

Interestingly the Egyptians rebuffed Aref's offer that their countries unify. When Nasser took over in Egypt he espoused Arab socialism; in effect he set up a *dirigiste* economy. Then, in 1958, he sought to form a union with Syria, and the scheme miscarried, in part because the free enterprise-minded Syrians balked at adopting *dirigisme*. Once burnt twice shy; so Nasser advised Aref (when the latter put forth the idea of their countries unifying) to overhaul Iraq's economy to bring it more in line with that of the Egyptians, and then they would consider a union.

This, Aref found impossible to do. Aref, a devout Muslim, was a conservative: unlike Qasem, he believed in property rights, and thus was unwilling to consider wholesale sequestration of privately held businesses, which is what had gone on in Egypt. Aref perished in a helicopter accident in 1966. While he lasted he went so far as to initiate a cautious opening to the West, a move closely watched by the Americans.

Aref's brother, Abdul Rahman, also a military man, then became president, and he continued the tentative movement into the western camp. However, in 1967 the Arab-Israeli war erupted, and violence (which, as I said, had merely been tamped down in Iraq) flared anew, as Iraqis took to the streets in protest. Perhaps in reaction to America's unequivocal support of Israel, Abdul Rahman resumed the oil nationalization, a process which had been allowed to lapse under the first Aref.

In July 1968, the second Aref was overthrown in a coup, instituted, he claimed, by the CIA. This probably is correct.[32] However, in Iraq, where things rarely seem to work out as planned, the coup miscarried, egregiously; in fact, it turned into a farce. Among the coup plotters were officer members of the Ba'th. These Ba'thists apparently did not know that one of the principals in the coup (indeed the man slated to become prime minister in the new government) was an officer whom they suspected of being an agent of the CIA, Abdul Razzaq al Nayef.[33] The Ba'thists caucused, and for a time, considered abstaining from the plot, but then deviously decided to go ahead. The coup came off. Once successful, the Ba'thists turned on Nayef. They packed him off to exile in Beirut. He later moved on to London (where the Ba'thists ultimately tracked him down and assassinated him, having been led to conclude that he was colluding with the British to return to power).[34]

Effectively then the Ba'thists had changed their stripes. Originally they were fiercely anti-Communist and pro-West—or at least were disposed to cooperate with the Americans (through the CIA). These second generation Ba'thists, however, not only dumped Nayef but also immediately on taking power they placed on trial a number of individuals whom they linked to the CIA; 29 of whom they hung. This action received wide publicity in the West, in part because among the executed were a number of Jews, whom the Ba'thists claimed were Zionists acting as agents for the CIA. Whatever hope the new regime might have had of gaining international acceptance was doomed after this. The stereotype of the Iraqis as pariahs was even more widely perceived.

Why did the Ba'thists perform in this way? To understand that one has to look back to the period of the 1960s. The 1967 War had just come off and Arab nationalism had been rudely checked. Nasser was driven to offer to resign, a move which was only thwarted by an outpouring of popular support among the Egyptians. Nonetheless, overnight the Arab nationalist cause was seen to have been compromised, and Arab nationalists every-where were stung. The Ba'thists clearly were registering this discomfort. They saw the Arab world as victimized by an imperialist-Zionist plot, in which the Americans were involved and so they cut ties to the West. Cut them in a big way, since they obviously put themselves beyond the pale with their actions.

In the face of this worldwide revulsion, the Ba'thists professed indiffer-ence. Indeed by their subsequent actions they seemed to have been staking out a position for themselves as the most radical of the Arab nationalist alignment—more anti-Israel, more anti-imperialist—and most novel— more anti-sheikh (they professed to despise the Arabs of the lower Gulf) than anyone.

The second coming of the Ba'th is of interest chiefly as it ushers in Hussein. At this point he was a soldier in the movement. However, he was also a relative of the new leader of Iraq, General Ahmed Hasan al Bakr, and Bakr reposed considerable trust in the youthful Saddam—he became Bakr's henchman. The general put him in charge of the so-called Public Relations Committee, which was meant to tackle subversion in Iraq.

Hussein did this by instituting a rule of repression, which even in Iraq was unprecedented. However, he did not merely have recourse to violent means. He acted more sophisticatedly. Hussein was instrumental in getting Bakr to enlist the aid of the East Germans. East Germany in those days faced many of the same problems as Iraq, with a population whose loyalty could not be counted on. Thus there came into being the so-called *Staatssicherheit* (Stasi), a secret police outfit. Wielding the Stasi as a tool, the East German government was able to suppress dissent at home. The Stasi's trick was to put huge numbers of East Germans on the payroll of the security forces, there to spy on their fellow Germans.

This was the method that Hussein adopted. He brought in the Stasi and effectively turned over the already existing Mukhabarat (secret police) to it. The East Germans converted the Mukhabarat into the most efficient security force in the Middle East. As the man behind the Mukhabarat—meaning the one who maintained the Ba'th in power—Hussein's influence increased exponentially. This prepared the way for the civilian element of the Ba'th to gain control over the military, because Hussein not only honeycombed the society at large with spies, he similarly infiltrated the military.

So it was not long before Hussein became the strongman ruler in Iraq, even though he was merely the Number Two behind Bakr. Bakr next appointed him to head up something called the Follow Up Committee, an organization created to complete the oil nationalization, which had been progressing fitfully under Abdul Rahman.[35] Hussein's breakthrough, that which moved the nationalization forward, was to solve the distribution problem. In 1950, the Iranians, under then-prime minister Mohammad Mossadeq, had nationalized their oil industry, only to have the nationalization fail because, although the Iranians controlled the oil, they could not market it. The oil cartel (the legendary Seven Sisters) monopolized the worldwide oil marketing and distribution system.

To clear this hurdle, Hussein worked out barter arrangements with the Russians, whereby in return for free oil from Iraq, the Communists undertook providing the Iraqis with much needed infrastructure. (The Soviets gained hard currency, which they got by selling Iraq's oil to their satellites.) The big oil companies had consistently over the years neglected Iraq's oil industry in preference to that of the Shah.[36] Consequently, Iraq had one of the largest oil reserves in the world, but not much production capacity; indeed because of this neglect Iraq continued to be a backward, impoverished country—until the Ba'th came along.

I do not think that anyone knows how much influence Hussein had in moving Iraq's society in the direction of collectivism. But I do think it noteworthy that Hussein, in forcing through the oil nationalization, turned for a solution to the Soviet Union, a collectivist society.

Under the Ba'th we see the whole of Iraq's economy gradually, but relentlessly, become collectivized. This is not an economic history of Iraq, so we need not go any further into this—except to note the following. As the society became more and more collectivized the bureaucracy naturally had to expand and this posed another big problem for the Ba'thists: how to keep control over this burgeoning apparatus?

Again, thanks to Hussein, Iraq was able to finesse this problem. As I said above, he had allowed the Stasi to overhaul the Mukhabarat, and thus had infiltrated the society with Mukhabarat agents. Now he expanded the process, turning the Mukhabarat loose on the bureaucracy, until, in effect, Iraq became one big police state.[37] Effectively the government put masses of Iraqis on the payroll as informants (the Stasi method.) This tied them to the Ba'th, since they now looked to it either for pay or favors, which (thanks to the OPEC revolution) the party was in a position to bestow.

There was a consequence (probably unintended) of this: the state became legitimated since it gained a monopoly over violence. Whereas before criminality was rampant, now that practically disappeared. And it is partially because of this that the Iraqi Mukabarat gained its fierce reputation. In the Middle East there is not a government that has not gotten its equivalent of the Mukhabarat. What is important is its effectiveness. In Iraq it was very effective.

Lest the reader subscribe to the popular wisdom view of the Ba'th as ruling solely by coercion, he/she should note the following: after the 1973 Arab oil embargo, followed by the OPEC Revolution, the lifestyle of Iraqis improved immensely. The Ba'th passed a number of pieces of legislation benefiting the underclass. For example,

> They forebade the expulsion of peasants from the land in any circumstances; abolished the right of the landlord under the Agrarian Reform Law to retain the best land; reduced the maximum limit of agricultural holdings... and did away with the principle of compensation for expropriated estates, thus freeing the peasants from redemption payments....They also introduced health insurance in the countryside, and launched massive programs for raising the cultural level of the rural population, the mechanization of agriculture, the electrification of about 4,200 villages and reclamation [of land]. In addition they created "peoples markets," enabling the peasants to sell the products of their labor at market prices through appropriate government agencies...without the interposition of middle men. Over and above this they maintained by state subsidy the price of the popular loaf of bread... lowered the price of all agricultural machines significantly and of chemical fertilizers...reduced the fees for state technical and advisory services... raised the minimum daily wage...extended social security and disability benefits.[38]

And in doing all of this, the Ba'thists primarily benefitted the Shias. Because, after all, they were the peasants. The Kurds did not benefit because the aghas successfully resisted imposition of the reforms, a stance which was aided by the Barzani revolt (which I will go into below): the revolt kept the North in a constant state of turmoil.

The Shias of the South had the best of times under the Ba'th, and this is something the Americans overlooked in planning their invasion where they counted on the Shias rising against the Ba'th. Why should they—the Ba'th had done well by them.

Through it all probably the chief reform the Ba'th put through involved education. The Ba'th instituted universal literacy, and that was an accomplishment of such scope, it was recognized by the United Nations.[39] Iraqis were encouraged to aim for college, all expenses paid by the government, largesse the government could afford because, again, after the OPEC revolution, petro dollars flooded the country.

Another innovation (this one specifically of Hussein) was to open the country to imported goods. Previously, the Ba'thists had imposed austerity; Hussein reversed this policy, which ingratiated him to the people, who now for the first time could indulge consumerist tendencies.[40] Hussein also attempted to turn the Ba'th, previously a vanguard party, into a mass movement. He removed many of the old line Ba'thists, enrolling a new generation of Iraqis into party ranks. This conciliated the youth because they now could hope to become part of the power structure—as Ba'thists, they could rise in society's ranks and conceive of themselves as (the Americans say) stake holders. Effectively an old, entrenched elite was being eliminated, giving way to a rising generation, and what is most interesting is the way to the top lay through the bureaucracy, a development similar to what took place in the Soviet Union.

The purge of the old line Ba'thists is frequently cited as an instance of Hussein's brutality, because in the process of removing the veterans he executed 21 of them. He accused them of plotting to take Iraq into union with Syria. What I find significant is Hussein's rationale for his having so acted. Had Iraq joined with Syria, it would then have been thrust into the Arab-Israeli conflict, in which Syria in those days was totally embroiled (it was in 1979 that Hussein did this). Hussein did not want Iraq's development drained by having to pour resources into that fight. A pragmatic stance to be sure, but one that affected Iraq profoundly. It became, for the first time in its history, a truly Gulf state. Under the Hashemites, and then under republicans like Aref, the face of Iraq continually was turned westward. The Hashemites tried several times to effect a union with Jordan (ruled by another Hashemite). Aref, the reader will recall, sought to unite with Egypt. One could say that Hussein was aping Qasem in striving to develop Iraq for the Iraqis.[41]

And this seemed to suit the Iraqis. One of the problems which the Arab nationalists never seemed to take into account, but which always made trouble for them, was that most Iraqis did not want to unite—not with another predominantly Sunni Arab country. The Shias had no interest in that and neither did the Kurds. Hussein, by frustrating Bakr's move to effect yet one more unification scheme, relieved a lot of minds of people who could only lose out in the process.

Going into the 1980s life in Iraq was good—for those who stayed out of politics, or at least avoided the wrong kind of politics. Hussein's policy was one of the carrot and the stick: as long as you did not get out of line politically, you might expect to be taken care of. Jobs were on offer in the bureaucracy; university education was open to all (including women), and most spectacularly everywhere were public works projects underway, as the Ba'thists poured petro dollars into developing infrastructure.

Most of these changes were effected behind a wall of secrecy. Iraq under the successive republican regimes was not open to the West. The United States, for example, had no embassy there after 1967. Iraq was a closed society, something on the order of North Korea today. But of course the big difference was that Iraq had money, which rolled in thanks to the oil. And of course, insofar as the Ba'thists sought to modernize Iraq, they had to open up somewhat to the outside world, bringing in contractors and the like.

In any event, here we have an introduction to Hussein's early history with the Ba'th. I now want to look at how he related to the army.

The Iraqi army's performance under the Ba'th (at least in the early years) was not stellar. The army participated in the 1973 Arab-Israeli War, but opinions differ as to how valuable the Iraqi contribution actually proved.[42] Moreover, when the Egyptians and Syrians agreed on a truce in that war, the Iraqis—disapproving of concessions—refused to sign, which meant that, after the 1973 conflict had ended, Iraq along with South Yemen remained at war with the Jewish state.

To be sure, the Iraqi army had a long history (from 1961) of fighting the rebellion of Mulla Mustafa Barzani, the Kurdish leader, in the North of Iraq. However, the consecutive assaults by Iraqi forces on the northern stronghold of Barzani always ended inconclusively. The Iraqi army (except on one occasion)[43] never fought through the winter, and, as a result, the Barzanis, taking advantage of the difficult terrain in the North, could always hold out till the snows came, when the plains-dwelling Arabs would return to the South.

Part of the officers' problem was the strained relations between them and Hussein: he did not trust them. Given the history of the army, its frequent interventions in government and its predisposition to intrigue, the mistrust no doubt was merited. However, as Hussein waxed more and more powerful, putting more and more of his people into positions of authority, he correspondingly constrained the activity of the officers.[44] When, for example, the Iraqi army went to war against Iran in 1980, the units were larded with the equivalent of Soviet-style commissars: Ba'th party loyalists, whose job it was to spy on the officers. There were instances of commissars countermanding orders of the officers in charge.

Along with not trusting the officers, Hussein—and his fellow Revolutionary Command Council (RCC) collegues[45]— had doubts about the rank and file soldiers. All throughout the Iran-Iraq war 65 percent of the regular army comprised Shias. The fear of the Ba'thists (initially) was that these would go over to the side of their co-religionists from Iran.[46] To guard against this, Popular Army men, whose loyalty was beyond dispute, were assigned to units alongside the regulars, supposedly there to provide stiffening to the Shias in the crush of battle (and also perhaps to shoot them, were they perceived to waver).

With so much mistrust of the troops, how could Iraq have gone to war with Iran (in 1980)? What would have motivated Hussein to launch an invasion of his neighbor in a situation such as this?

The popular belief (at least in the West) is that the Iraqis initiated the war; that it was a kind a sneak attack they perpetrated. It was hardly that. The run up to the war was a long time unfolding: successive clashes marked the development of hostilities. Indeed there was a period when all along the frontier artillery duels erupted daily (this, before the war was declared). Conditions inside Iraq provoked the confrontation: Khomeini had for some time been fomenting rebellion. It was the aim of the Iranians under Khomeini "to export the revolution," which they did, not just to Lebanon—the famous case—but also to Bahrain, an attempt which failed notably, and also to Saudi Arabia. Attempts were made to sew dissension among Saudi Arabia's Shia community in the far eastern area of the peninsula (where some of the biggest oil field are located). In the case of Iraq, the Iranian leader agitated both in the North among the Iraqi Kurds and in southern lands of the Shias.[47]

Hussein had it in mind that he was going to fight a limited war; his aim was to seize the Iranian province of Khuzestan, heavily populated with Arab Iranians.[48] He would hold it to exact concessions from Khomeini, concessions which Hussein felt were due. In 1975, in clashes between the forces of the Shah of Iran and the Ba'thists, Iraq and Iran had come perilously close to war; however, they drew back. (This was the Barzani revolt, to which I have already made reference; the Shah backed the Barzanis, indeed he put them up to revolting).[49] As part of the negotiated settlement, Iraq surrendered sovereignty over half the Shatt al Arab, the waterway connecting Basrah—Iraq's second city, and its only real port—to the Gulf. It did this in return for the Shah's promise to discontinue aiding the rebellion of the Barzani Kurds. The Shah also agreed to relinquish certain tracts of land along the shared border. However, when in 1979 the Shah was overthrown that territory still had not been returned. Khomeini refused to honor the agreement, and along with that he resumed intriguing with the Kurds. Hussein's intention, therefore, was to seize the southernmost province of

Iran on the Gulf, and hold it until Iran handed over the disputed territories and quit intriguing with the Kurds.[50]

In the opening phase of the Iran-Iraq War, the Iraqi army fought well, extremely well given the difficulties with which it was beset. The officers' chief headache was Hussein's micromanaging of the conflict. For example, he kept ordering halts to the campaign. The Iraqi army would attack and gain ground. Then Hussein—through the agency of the United Nations— would call a truce, which the Iranians would refuse to accept. Then, the officers would have to gear up and go at it all over again.

Despite this fitful carrying on of the war, which effectively robbed the Iraqi commanders of crucial momentum, in the first months the army was able to seize a major Iranian city, Khoramshah. This was the first instance (after World War II) of a major city in the Middle East falling in wartime. The Israelis never were able to do as much—they never did take Beirut. Indeed, military men, generally, regard the capture of a major city—one that is actively defended—as no mean feat. (This operation is also significant inasmuch as it shows the Iraqi army as far back as this had experience with urban warfare, which, as I will show, it is now conducting against the United States.)

The Iraqis also won the battle of Susangard, the biggest tank battle to have been fought not just in the Middle East but anywhere post-World War II, until the first Iraq War. The Iranian prime minister, Bani Sadr, had been directing the Iranian forces up till this point. After the Iranians' defeat at Susangard he was relieved of command by Khomeini, and subsequently he fled to Europe.

After Susangard, the Revolutionary Guards (the toughs I referred to above) took over the Iranian forces, with which the tide of battle turned. The Guards instituted the tactic of the human wave attack where they flung masses of infantry at the Iraqi line, expending lives prodigally as they sought a breakthrough, which they eventually did achieve.

It was the Iraqi Popular Army men who funked it. There they were embedded among the Shias so as to keep the latter from defecting. These ex-street fighters—now jumped-up bureaucrats—were full of themselves. They believed they could fight, but, in fact, from a military standpoint, they were next to worthless: they lacked discipline; the professional military men despaired of them.

The human wave attacks, I am told by those who have witnessed them, are awesome. Masses of humanity screaming fanatically come on over the corpses of their fallen comrades. Nothing can check the advance—at least so it must have seemed to the Popular Army men, who promptly cracked. Horror stricken, they threw down their arms and either surrendered en masse, or fled.[51] This resulted in whole units decomposing. It was not long after this that the Iraqis fell back to the border. The collapse commenced in 1982, two years into the war. By the summer of that year, opinion among analysts in the West was that the fight was over: Basrah would be taken; Iraq would certainly lose the war.

It never happened. Outside Basrah, the Iraqis regrouped and held. Moreover in repelling the Iranians they inflicted dreadful losses on their enemy.[52] This turnabout impressed western intelligence. To explain it the theory was advanced that the Iraqis, while no good on the offense, were formidable when fighting in defense of their homeland. It is a notable assessment, because it implies that which the Americans later denied: that the Shias (who after all were the bulk of the army) had some national sentiment.

There was a big boost to come out of this for the Iraqi army. After it had held at Basrah, Hussein called in Egyptian officers to critique its performance. The Egyptians suggested a number of reforms which, they said, should be implemented immediately. The most interesting for our purposes was this. The Iraqis, according to the Egyptians, had to develop a serious military intelligence capability. To be sure the Iraqis had such, or thought they did. It was presided over by Hussein's half brother, Barzan, which meant that it was part of the Mukhabarat, Barzan's balliwick. Barzan's idea of what an intelligence service should do was to spy on the officers.

That, said the Egyptians, is not what military intelligence is supposed to be about. Getting Barzan to relinquish control over military intelligence was not an easy proposition. He resisted, enlisting two other half brothers of Hussein (Watban and Sabawi) in support.

This power struggle was keenly observed in the West, where the Mukhabarat was seen as the mainstay of the regime; thus it was presumed that, were Barzan (who indisputably led the Mukhabarat) to have fallen out with Hussein, this could only presage the end of the Ba'th. However, the matter was resolved: the conduct of military intelligence was turned over to the army and Barzan was relieved of his directorship of the Mukhabarat, after which he was posted to Switzerland where he became Iraq's ambassador.[53]

This, in my view, marks the beginning of the Iraqi army's freeing itself from civilian control, and becoming a professional fighting force. As long as commissars reporting to the Mukhabarat were embedded in the units, obviously the officers' freedom of action was curtailed.

Something else happened in this period which also had an effect on the conduct of the war and on the development of the army. Ronald Reagan dispatched U.S. Congressman Stephen Solarz to Baghdad to sound out the Iraqis about curbing Iraq's anti-Israel stance.[54] Which Iraq more or less did, and in return the United States abandoned its neutrality and came over to Iraq's side in the war.[55] The Americans agreed to start a campaign in the United Nations to bring about a peaceful, negotiated conclusion to the fighting. In making the switch to cooperate with the Americans, the Ba'thists were shifting their stance yet again. Not only did Hussein open the country up to contact with Washington, but he also made a similar opening to the Gulf sheikhs. I noted above that the Ba'thists disdained the sheikhs, looking on them as retrogressive. Under Hussein that attitude changed. Which was fortunate, as the Iraqis were becoming desperately in need of financial assistance, which the sheikhs of course were in a position to supply.

A point about this aid: The sheikhs expected it would be used exclusively to buy weapons. In the early part of the war, Iraq had funded such expenses by selling off gold reserves; however, as the war dragged on these became exhausted. When the sheikhs agreed to take over the funding for arms purchases, Hussein diverted some of this aid to the civilian sector. Thus he was able to pursue a guns-and-butter policy.[56] And this enabled Iraqis to maintain their comfortable lifestyles throughout pretty much all of the war. And of course this has bearing on the attitude of the Shias toward the government. Had Hussein imposed austerity measures, and not kept on aggrandizing them, they might have turned on him. By continuing largesse, he kept them reasonably happy. To be sure they had to fight (as I said 65 percent of the army was Shia), but the manner in which the war was waged was unusual. Essentially there was one big battle every year, year after year. The Iranians would mobilize and throw themselves at Basrah (the usual target); the Ba'thists would strive to resist. The battles sometimes would go on for weeks, but in the end, once repulsed, the Iranians would withdraw to mobilize for next year's event: among the western intelligence community these were referred to as the "rainy season bashes," because they usually came off in February, during the rainy season.

The Shias, assuming they survived the one big blood letting, could expect to return to living more or less normally, until the next go round, so to speak. This has bearing on claims, often heard in the West, that Hussein's war inflicted great pain on Iraqis: the war was costly, but the costs could be borne under the circumstances.[57]

When I visited Iraq in 1984 (as an intelligence officer) I was struck by the mood in Baghdad—you could not tell there was a war going on. The fighting raged within a few miles of the capital but Iraqis went about their lives as if peace prevailed. The shops were well stocked; the daily routine seemed normal.

And as for the actual conduct of the war, there was a big change there also. Buoyed by outside support, Hussein (and the RCC) adopted a stance of fighting the war along the lines of static defense. The Iraqi army settled down to holding the line; keeping the Iranians in check, while the United States presumably concentrated, in the United Nations, on trying to broker a truce.[58]

The Iraqis are excellent engineers. Their defense works (according to American officers who inspected them) were impressive. Professional military men on the Iranian side might have devised means of overcoming them, but the Iranians had no such thing as a general staff.[59] The Revolutionary Guards ran the show, and these Guardsmen (as I said) were—like the

Popular Army men in Iraq—originally street toughs. The Guards had only one tactic: the human wave attack, which was fairly primitive: essentially it consisted of throwing untrained recruits at well defended positions.[60] As a consequence Iran suffered enormous casualties; but given that the Iranians outnumbered the Iraqis three to one, they evidently felt they could sustain such losses.

The Iranians' ace-in-the-hole (they felt) was the putative uncertain loyalty of the Iraqi Shias. The Iraqi army, as I said, comprised 65 percent Shias, and these co-religionists were subjected to constant propagandizing by the Islamists, who called on them, in effect, to rally to the faith; abandon their support for the infidel Ba'thists and come over to the side of Iran. The organization, on the Iranian side, that directed the propaganda effort was the Supreme Council of the Islamic Revolution in Iraq (SCIRI), directed then, as it is now, by the Hakim brothers. The older brother, Muhammad Bakr al Hakim, was an ayatollah, from a family long prominent in religious circles in Iraq. Indeed he was a rival of Muhammad Bakr al Sadr (of whom I speak in the next chapter). Whereas the Sadrs stayed put in Iraq, the Hakims fled, and this becomes a matter of importance later under the American occupation when the Iranians send SCIRI back to Iraq to constitute an Iranian Fifth Column.

Muhammad Baker's brother, Abdul Aziz, headed Dawa, which at that time was the military arm of SCIRI. Dawa carried out terror operations in Iraq, until Hussein rounded up all of the Hakims who resided there and threatened to kill them one by one unless Dawa desisted, which it did. The group later switched operations, perpetrating terror operations in the Gulf. It blew up the American embassy in Kuwait in 1983. Like SCIRI, Dawa also returned to Iraq when the occupation was set up, and a member of Dawa became Iraq's first prime minister under the fledgling American-sponsored government in Iraq.

SCIRI's mission of subverting Iraqi Shias was a notable failure. The Iraqi Shias did not budge in their loyalty, and the Iranians were so incensed by this, as they viewed it, tergiversation, they massacred Iraqi Shias who fell into their hands. In fighting in 1983 numerous Iraqi corpses were discovered mutilated by the Iranians.[61]

I think the significance of this failure cannot be overemphasized. One of the biggest mistakes the Bush administration made in planning for its Iraq adventure was to assume that the Iraqi Shias were Shias first and only incidentally Iraqis. The resoluteness displayed in the Iran-Iraq War contradicts this. The Shias had no love for the Iranians, and, I would argue, they also exhibited (at this stage) a rudimentary loyalty to their country.

One other thing happened as a result of the Iranians' attempts to score a breakthrough against Basrah. The following year, casualties on both sides skyrocketed, but the Iraqis were most affected because of the circumstance of how the Popular Army was set up. As is the case in the United States with the National Guard, Popular Army units reported by region: individuals from a specific locality served together at the front. As a consequence, when the fight waxed fierce whole units could be (and in this case were) decimated. This in turn redounded adversely on the welfare of the communities whence they derived. A number of Iraqi villages saw practically their whole complement of young males eradicated. So terrible was the loss, the Ba'thists actually refused to send bodies home for burial, fearing a morale collapse. They stored them in freezer lockers, releasing them piecemeal.[62]

At any rate, as a result of this fiasco, Hussein ordered the Popular Army units withdrawn from frontline service, whence they retired to the northern Kurdish areas, essentially to do patrol duty there.[63] I went to the North of Iraq in 1984 and saw them in operation. Among the regular army men I spoke with, the Popular Army units were regarded as awkward squads.

This withdrawal of the Popular Army men was another plus for the professional military. The Popular Army had been all along a thorn in the officers' sides, and thus Hussein, by withdrawing the units, did the army a favor. At the same time he eroded somewhat the party's power because the Popular Army was the party's "thing," so to speak—an institution it specifically wielded (along with the Mukhabarat) as a check on the military.

It was after this that the Iranians abandoned their regular assaults on Basrah and began instead to seek a breakthrough elsewhere along the border. This change put enormous strains on the much smaller Iraqi army, which barely could respond to sudden, unanticipated incursions that might develop anywhere along the line. Here is where the Americans were able to help out.

The CIA began supplying satellite photos of the Iranian buildups along the frontier.[64] By studying the photos, which the CIA regularly delivered to the Iraqis in Baghdad (the Americans had reestablished diplomatic relations with Iraq in 1984 and opened an Interests Section in the capital), the Iraqi commanders were able to reinforce quickly anywhere along the front. The Iraqis were forewarned, in other words, by the Americans as to where the attacks would likely come.

The Iraqi general in charge at this point was Hisham al Fakhri, a good officer (according to the American military attaches). It was Fakhri who conceived the idea of converting the Republican Guards. Previously the Guards had been a mere ceremonial unit which never left Baghdad. But Fakhri converted it into a commando force. In addition he ordered roads built all along the border. This way the Iraqis could speed Guards units to anywhere on the frontier so as to repel the Iranian breakthroughs.

Since 1983 the Iraqis had been experimenting with the use of chemicals.[65] The Iranians' chief assault tactic was (as I said) the human wave attack. Gas is not a weapon of mass destruction (WMD) (more about this later), but it is an excellent means of instilling panic in attacking units. This was how it was used by combatants in World War I, to break up attacks in the trench warfare phase. Just so, the Iraqis used gas to break up the Iranians' headlong assaults.

Fakhri, however, used the gas in a more sophisticated manner. For example, in 1985, during the battle of Badr, which took place in the southern marshes near Majnoon, Fakhri allowed the Revolutionary Guards to penetrate deep into the swamp on the Iraqi side, then dropped chemicals behind them, trapping the disoriented Iranians in a kind of kill box, where they were destroyed.[66]

It is likely more than one of these innovations (of Fakhri) came from the Americans. Up to this point in the conflict both sides, Iraqi and Iranian, pursued a primitive style of warfare where they concentrated on seizing territory. It is the American style of war to kill as many of the opposing forces as possible—total war, in other words; indeed, this is what modern war essentially is about.

The Reagan administration had stationed military attaches in Baghdad, who (although this was never their purpose) mentored the Iraqis, schooling them in the lessons of modern warfare (I know this because I talked with officers who told me that they found the Iraqis extremely apt pupils.) It took time but the Iraqis eventually came to see that, for them, the aim of war should be to wipe the enemy out, *destroy him;* they should maneuver to obtain the highest kill-ratios possible, and that is what they now began to do.

By 1985, it was the belief of the intelligence community in Washington that Iraq had turned the corner in the war; the battle was now going in its favor. Unless something untoward developed, the Iraqis were going to win. Then came the ill-fated battle of Al Faw, an event that very much needs to be put into context.

The Israelis, as I noted earlier, had at one point entertained the notion of improving relations with the Ba'thists.[67] They saw in Hussein a pragmatist whom they hoped to wean away from uncompromising hostility to the Jewish state. And indeed Hussein somewhat confirmed this view when he made the aforementioned concessions to Solarz. However, when Itzak Shamir came to power in Israel attitudes changed. Shamir was a proponent of what subsequently became known as the Likud Doctrine, whereby the Israelis eschewed co-existence with the Arabs, and aimed for total subjugation. Thus sometime in 1985, the Israelis began plotting to sabotage the Americans' accord with Baghdad; they sought not just to end cooperation between Washington and Iraq but also to, in effect, get the Americans to switch allegiance to Tehran. And they did this through the medium of arms sales.

Israel had been covertly supplying the Iranians with arms (at a price) since the outbreak of the Iran-Iraq War.[68] The Shah's army had been equipped by the Americans and, as a consequence, the Khomeiniists were acutely embarrassed when, after inciting the hostility of Washington (through their hostage seizure),[69] they found they could not get spare parts for their weapons. Israel, which regularly was supplied with arms by the Americans, had a surplus and thus was motivated to cash in on the potentially lucrative arms traffic with the Islamic Republic.[70]

This of course was against American law. A state like Israel which receives weapons (gratis) from the United States cannot then turn around and sell them to a third party, especially a state with whom the United States is inimical.[71] Until roughly 1983–1984 it is likely that, although the Americans were aware of the clandestine arms trading, they were indisposed to make a fuss. But, then, in 1983, the Israelis invaded Lebanon, where, after a number of dazzling early successes, they ultimately bogged down. Ariel Sharon, the defense minister at the time, aimed to take Beirut, the Lebanese capital, after which he and the Israeli Prime Minister Menahim Begin entertained the grandiose scheme of flipping the Lebanese, taking them out of the Arab camp and turning that tiny—but strategically important country—into an ally of Israel.

A breathtaking conception, but like a lot of grand schemes this one was wildly impractical. The Lebanese, who were bitterly opposed to the Palestinians, nonetheless were Lebanese—they had no intention of becoming a satellite of the Israelis. A number of heavy handed moves by Sharon excited anger in important sectors of the Lebanese community. Most notably the Lebanese Shia and Druze shifted not to the side of the Palestinians but against the Israelis.

Reagan, in an attempt to extricate the Israeli Defense Force (IDF) from its bogged-down condition in Lebanon, sent U.S. troops to the Levant, the intention being to interpose the Americans between the hostile Lebanese and the Israelis. Robert McFarland, who was the national security advisor at the time, made a number of ill-considered moves that convinced the anti-Israeli Lebanese that the Americans were not the honest broker they claimed to be but were rather secretly aiding the Jewish state.

In 1983, the infamous destruction of the Marine Corps barracks at Beirut occurred, in which 233 U.S. Marines perished. The barracks had been blown up by a suicide truck bomber, a Shia. The Shias then followed that up with a similar attack on the headquarters of the French peacekeepers, and topped it off by blowing up the headquarters of the IDF.

In the United States, public opinion, which until then had been indifferent about the Iran-Iraq war, swung massively over to the side of opposing the Iranians (a natural response, since it was widely credited that the Lebanese Shias were clients of the Islamic Republic). This put the Israelis, with their covert arms sales to Tehran, in an awkward position. If the sales became public (as they could easily have done; they were common knowledge within the American intelligence community), relations between the Jewish state and its number one protector might have been jeopardized.

Not wanting to lose the revenue from the sales, and also keen to keep the Iranians in the war against Iraq (partly, as I said, because Shamir was an inveterate Iraq hater), the Israelis conceived the idea of placing the arms sales on a new basis: they would renounce the revenue from the sales—indeed they would divert the cash to the Nicaraguan Contras.[72] This was another audacious conception; in certain respects it was ingenious. William Casey, the head of the CIA under Reagan, was cranked (or so we in the community felt) on "winning one back from the ruskies"; Casey wanted to co-opt a Russian satellite into the American camp.

The Israelis claimed that doing a deal with Tehran could achieve two laudable ends. On the one hand, it would divert much-needed cash to the Contras,[73] but also, the Israelis proposed to intervene in Tehran to get the Iranians to pressure Hizbollah, their client, to release a number of American hostages the Hizbollahis were holding.

Reagan went along with this. However the Americans (and the Iranians) insisted on keeping the transaction over the arms deal secret. It all got out, however, when an obscure paper in Lebanon blew the story, and Iran's prime minister Hashemi Rafsanjani, confronted by enemies in Tehran, was forced to own up.

One can imagine the shock of the Iraqis, who had thought that they had a deal with the Americans, indeed, that the Americans were on their side. Iraq was pursuing its static defense strategy; holding the line against Iran, patiently waiting for the Americans to bring about a negotiated settlement. Now they discovered it was all a ramp: the Americans had gone over to the enemy. And that left the Iraqis *precisely where?*

Not only were the Americans supplying the Iranians with weapons, but they also, it developed, had fed the Iraqis doctored satellite photos, which had led them to expect an Iranian attack in one part of the front, while secretly the Iranians (with American connivance) were building up to attack at Al Faw.[74]

The loss of Al Faw, which came in late 1986, stunned the Iraqis because this was a major city.[75] Iraq's whole strategy had been to prevent Iran from achieving any big breakthroughs, and now the Iranians had done precisely that. Moreover, TOW (anti-tank) missiles and Hawk batteries, which were instrumental in enabling the Iranians to succeed in this operation, had been supplied to Tehran as part of the surreptitious Iran/Contra arms deal.

Reagan's prestige was seriously damaged over the so-called Iran/Contra scandal; his fumbling attempts to put a good face on the transaction were disastrous. The Iraqis could take heart from the fact that, so great was Reagan's embarrassment, any possibility of further cooperation between the Americans and Iranians was precluded (that is, it was immediately so; we will see how the Americans reverted to the Iranians' side eventually).

But still the Iraqis were one down in the war; that is, the move towards a negotiated settlement had stalled—more than stalled, it was dead in the water. That summer—the summer of 1986—the Ba'thists met in a secret session in Baghdad, in which the Iraqi general staff made the case to Hussein that the strategy of static defense was no longer operable.[76] The army would have to take the offensive, the generals said. It was the only way, not just to win the war but also to survive it, as the generals recognized that, in a no-win situation, they would be slowly bled to death.

All very well, but to take the offensive, the Iraqi generals *would have to be given charge of the war-fighting.* In other words, *Saddam Hussein was going to have to give up his micromanaging.* You can micromanage with an army on the defense, but when it shifts to an offensive mode, decisions have to be made by the commanders at the front. Giving up control—which meant reposing trust in the military—was a big step for Hussein and his fellow RCC collegues.

To get an idea of how big, consider the following. Prior to 1986, the average Iraqi had virtually no idea whom were the generals conducting the war. The top officers never received publicity in the press. If an Iraqi commander won a great victory, he praised Hussein in his communique (which would be printed in the press without attribution; in other words, the general was never named). He would imply that the victory had come under Hussein's direction (this was Hussein, the civilian, who had never served in the military!).

It is interesting to view Hussein's handling of the army in light of modern management practices. Acting on precepts laid down by the Stasi, Hussein, had created a thoroughly bureaucratized state, in the course of which he had concomitantly bureaucratized the army. His intense monitoring of all aspects of the war-fighting had converted the military into a virtual bureau of the government. Now, one could say, Hussein was setting it free. By handing over direction of the conduct of the war to the officers, he abandoned Taylorism, making the military a practically autonomous (and certainly professional) institution.[77]

I mentioned Fakhri before, and said that, in the eyes of the American attaches, he was a more than competent commander. Iraq had another good officer: Abdul Maher Rashid. Rashid was the opposite of Fakhri (character wise). If Fakhri was colorless, stolid (he was a big man), Rashid was dapper and trim. Rashid was always well dressed and affected a marshal's baton. He also was known as a martinet, albeit a professional, a man who demanded and got absolute obedience, and who yet enjoyed the respect of his junior officers.[78]

Rashid was entrusted with the job of retaking Al Faw. A dirty, *dirty* job if there ever was one. Al Faw is stuck off on the end of a peninsula which juts into the Gulf. To reach it, one has to pass along a narrow corridor of land, bordered with Gulf water on one side, impassable swamp on the other.

At Hussein's command, Rashid took on the assignment of recapturing Al Faw, which developed into a veritable blood bath. Time and again, Rashid threw the Iraqi forces into the breach, to inch their way along the narrow spit of land, under the constant fire of the Iranians (who were being supplied from a base across the Shatt al Arab).

After days of this cruel, unrelenting punishment, Rashid concluded the job was hopeless. The best the Iraqis could do was to seal off the peninsula and get on with the war.

The Iraqis' position was now severely compromised. 1987 was coming, and the Iranians were advertising this as the year of the "Battle of Destiny": they were going to raise a million-man army to throw at Iraq. Not only would the greatly outnumbered Iraqis have to defend the city of Basrah (where the Iranian attack was spearheaded), they would as well have to keep the Iranians bottled up in Al Faw—a breakout by the Revolutionary Guards there would put the Iraqis in a pincers. Further, the Iranians were agitating with the Kurdish leader—Masoud Barzani, Mulla Mustafa's son—to open a second front in the North of Iraq. (It was this last development which, incidentally, provoked the Iraqis to step up their operations in the North against rebellious Kurds, which subsequently was held to be a campaign of genocide by the Americans; more about this in the next chapter.)

Rashid, Fakhri, and the other general staff officers devised a plan whereby Iraq would take the offensive. But not just like that. Having so long pursued a policy of static defense, the Iraqi army lacked the initiative, the *elan,* to go on the offensive. The generals were going to have to raise the equivalent of a new army. They decided to create additional Republican Guards units, and, for these, they wanted only the finest recruits.

Hussein agreed to a call-up, but he went about implementing it in a devious manner. Iraq already had a draft, but, as was the case with Americans in the Korean and Vietnam wars, it spared college students, who could claim exemption. Thus the brunt of the fighting was being borne by nonstudents. And since many of these tended to derive from the less well-to-do classes, the burden of defending the county fell unequally on those not so advantaged. Now, the RCC let it be known that university classes would be postponed. Students were going to have to go for military training. It was left open whether this was to be a bona fide draft. (It was intimated that the students might be able to resume classes in the fall; however, late.[79])

On the other hand, the RCC refused to be pinned down on this. They did say that those Iraqi youths who signed up for the Republican Guards units (which were now being referred to as the Golden Force) would be privileged. They would be Hussein's own, in a manner of speaking, making their families eligible for all sorts of perks.

In a society like that of Iraq, where practically all Iraqis were, one way or another, living off the state, to be put in a special relationship with Hussein was everything one could hope for; careerwise it opened up vast vistas of rewards. Of course those students who held back might find themselves drafted into the regular army, which was not at all an enviable alternative.

The Republican Guards slots were immediately filled, and the generals consequently were enabled to build up their new offensive force. At the U.S. Army War College, where I was then serving as a senior professor, we were able to show that the number of brigades in the Republican Guards was increased from 1983, when there were none, to six in 1987.[80] Obviously this innovation of expanding the Guard also affected the character of the army, which now became a more representative institution: with citizens of all classes filling the ranks it becomes, in respect to size (it numbered a million men), a veritable microcosm of the state.

All of this, by the way, was carried on *sub rosa*. Iraq, as I have said, was a closed society where secrets could be kept. To be sure, the Americans at the Interests Section in Baghdad were aware something was afoot, but nothing was ever definite; the outline of the plan remained obscure. Also, the Ba'thists did not make an issue of their betrayal over Iran/Contra. They continued to deal with the Americans, and also with the Gulf sheikhs—but in fact they had switched sides yet again, inasmuch as they now no longer trusted the Americans. They were going to try to end the war on their own.

In any event, the students went off to secret camps in the western desert. There, the recruits to the Guard units were drilled in various offensive maneuvers. Meanwhile weapons continued flowing into Iraq. All manner of materiel (paid for by the Saudis and Kuwaitis) was off-loaded at Kuwait City and driven north by truck. Much of the transport moved by night, to ensure concealment. And, of course, along with constituting new Guards units, the Iraqis stepped up mobilization generally, so that, essentially, two huge armies were in the process of forming, each with over a million men— all for this big battle the Iranians were set to launch in 1987. That the Iraqis, who (populationwise) were outnumbered three to one by the Iranians, could mobilize a million men was an extraordinary feat. It also said something about the Iraqis' commitment to the regime that the previously privileged college youth would allow themselves to be conscripted into the military.

On the Iranian side, the Revolutionary Guards recruited also, not only into the Revolutionary Guards but also the *basij,* which was the outfit which led the charge in the human wave attacks. In Iran, the net was being cast wider and wider: all across the country, whole villages were being called up, loaded onto trucks and transported to the western front. And, of course, sensitized by Tehran's propaganda (about the Battle Of Destiny) the Gulf became a magnet for foreign military observers and press. Everyone wanted to be in on this great event.

There was not just one Battle of Destiny: they were actually six. The first Iranian attempt at a breakthrough came at the most extreme southern part of the front at the Shatt al Arab on the night of December 26, 1986. The Iraqis stopped that one cold.[81]

Two weeks later, the Iranians shifted their attack a little farther north, to Fish Lake outside of Basrah. This, as it turned out, came to be the culminating (in a manner of speaking) battle of the Iran-Iraq War. This engagement was dubbed Karbala V. Here, the tactics worked out by the Iraqis are worth dilating upon.

The Iraqis created huge artificial sand berms, which they could move around. They then waited for the Iranian human wave attackers to launch. By positioning the berms, the Iraqis were able to channel the waves. They were facilitated in this by another maneuver: they electrified vast standing pools of water outside Basrah through which the Iranians had to pass. This had the effect of creating kill zones: whenever Iranians units strayed into one of the pools they would be electrocuted. Thus the Iraqis compelled the Iranians to divert their headlong charge along previously worked out paths, or channels. Never stopping, because of fear of losing momentum, the attackers coursed ahead. Meanwhile the Iraqis manipulated the attackers as a pinball operator works the game: deflecting the ball (the ball being the attackers) now this way, now that, all the while steering them into prese-lected areas—the kill zones. When finally the waves erupted full spate into the zones, the Iraqis closed them off and set about massacring the pent up forces. It is estimated the Iranians lost thousands in this battle alone.[82]

After Karbala V, Iran made other attempts to break through along the frontier. Essentially, though, the Battle of Destiny ended with Karbala V, and along with it the war. The Iranians lost so many troops in the spring/ summer of 1987 that they were unable to return to the fight (not with any convincing show of force) the following year.

So abrupt was the turnaround that the world outside of the Middle East could not assimilate it. If one goes back and reads accounts in papers like *The Washington Post* and *New York Times,* it is remarkable how the journalists failed to perceive the decisiveness of what had occurred. The perception (on the American side) was that the Iranians, by pushing their front line a few meters closer to Basrah, had positioned themselves to break through the following year.

In fact, the Iranian army had died that year in the sands outside of Basrah. The Iraqi army, I would say, had come into its own. Its triumph was practi-cally unalloyed. The Americans may not have appreciated this, but the Iraqis certainly did: to have beaten the Iranians—the Iran of the Shah, of the much-vaunted Islamic Revolution—this was something. I would say that it was this victory that first set Iraqis to thinking about themselves as Iraqis. After this, being an Iraqi, in their own minds, stood for something.

The actual end came in 1988, when the Iraqis launched a series of battles (*Tawakalna ala Allah*, in God We Trust) along the entire frontier, driving the Iranians out of territories they previously had occupied. In the final battle the Iraqis pushed many kilometers into Iran, and then stopped, by prearrangement, turning the action over to units of the Mujahadeen al Khalq, an anti-Khomeini Iranian group.[83] The idea was to let the opposi-tionists see what they could do. The Mujahadeen essentially did nothing, being balked by a stubborn defense put up by the Revolutionary Guards. In any event, that ended the war; Khomeini was forced to "drink the poison cup of defeat," as he put it.

What follows next is little understood by Americans, and yet I believe the fallout in relations between the United States and Iraq starts here. The Iraqis assumed that they would now enter into negotiations for a cessation of hostilities, and almost certainly they looked to impose a victor's peace. However, the Americans stepped in, effectively tying up the talks conducted by the United Nations. The United States backed Iran's refusal to engage in face-to-face discussions, which, for the Iraqis, was a sine qua non. Thus the negotiations stalled, and as they lapsed Hussein found himself stymied—he could not demobilize his troops, a fact which caused him immense difficulty.[84]

To pay for the war, Iraq had run up huge debts, the interest on which compounded at such a rate in no time it became impossible to meet payments. The situation was not helped when Kuwait announced that money Iraq thought had been given it in the form of grants was in fact a loan. Along with that, Kuwait and the United Arab Emirates (UAE) began throwing oil onto the market, driving down the price. Since oil revenue was the only means Iraq had of making payments, it faced bankruptcy.

Hussein claimed, in his famous interview with U.S. Ambassador April Glaspie,[85] that the United States was colluding with the sheikhs to destroy him economically. Hussein also made a barely veiled threat in that interview, to take drastic action unless the United States brought pressure on Kuwait and the UAE to reverse policy towards Iraq.

Glaspie either did not pick up on the threat (which is hard to credit) or else the diplomats back in Foggy Bottom failed to perceive the seriousness of what was at stake. As was proven, Hussein was not bluffing, for shortly after this the Iraqi army crossed the border and in a matter of hours Kuwait fell.

Why did the Americans do as they did? America never wanted a military solution in that war. Were either side to win militarily the power balance in the Gulf would be upset, and this would threaten American hegemony there. But also the Americans did not believe that the Iraqi army could take over Kuwait. The belief was that the army would take so long to mobilize, the United States would have ample opportunity to head it off. In any event, with, as far as I know, only one demurer, this was the collective wisdom of the American intelligence agencies.[86]

The agencies obviously had failed to cognize the transformation of the Iraqi military. The question then becomes, why did they? It is not so hard to figure out. The end of the war came over a period of two years. The beginning of the end, for Iran, came at Karbala V, when the Iranians lost so many men, trying to take Basrah, that they had difficulty recruiting for another mammoth offensive schedule for 1988.

When the Iraqis kicked off their Tawakalna campaign (in the spring of 1988), the Iranian front was depleted, although this was not perceived by observers at the time. Hence, they easily rolled up the Iranian line, forcing the defeat.

Not able to understand how the Iraqis could prove so effective—how, for example, they could have overwhelmed Al Faw in a mere four hours—analysts leapt to the wrong conclusion that they had used gas. Later on, when the Iraqis went into the North of Iraq to drive out the Barzani guerrillas and in the process relocate Kurdish villages away from the Iran border, the Americans leapt to another wrong conclusion that the Iraqis were using gas against the Kurds—hence genocide.[87]

These wrong analyses were to prove damaging to the Americans' cause when it came time to invade Iraq in 2003, since they believed by then that the Iraqi general staff had no proficiency but would resort to gas, to defend itself. Instead the generals had gone to the outside-in defense, using paramilitaries, which totally surprised the Americans and momentarily disoriented them.

3

Bad Intel

Up to this point I have been focusing on the growth of professionalism of the Iraqi army and I did this by way of preparing the reader for what will be one of the more important points I hope to make in the book: namely, that the Iraqi army—the old Ba'thist army—made the resistance which is now being carried on against the Americans. The officers—after they had been cashiered by America's proconsul L. Paul Bremer III (see below)— formed the resistance and by their exertions drove it in the early stages— until at a certain point, because of numerous mistakes the Americans made, the resistance took off becoming more widespread. In this chapter I discuss the origin of the resistance, but first we need to look at some of the attitudes the Americans brought with them to Iraq, because these influenced the course that the resistance took.

The Americans on going into Iraq lacked basic knowledge about the country and as a consequence were not equipped to manage the occupation. To a degree it was natural they would be so unknowing. As I said in the last chapter, Iraq under the Ba'th was a closed society, one where the government gave out scant information about what went on, and of course it never encouraged tourism so there were few in the United States who had been exposed to that society; hence the ignorance.[1]

Over and above this, however, there was a set of ideas the Americans held about Iraq which they had acquired from various sources over the years, and which originally may have been cogent but by 2003 (when the invasion took place) were very much out of date.[2]

This wrong intelligence, as I show, complicated attempts to work with the Iraqis under the occupation. Indeed some of the ideas were so wrong-headed they enflamed relations between natives and occupiers, and that specifically is what led to the revolt. There would not have been a revolt, if the Americans had not behaved so maladroitly.

We will see how this worked out when we come to discussing the actual operation of the resistance. Now we need to be clear as to what the wrong ideas were. In what areas were the Americans so misinformed, and which subsequently got them into such trouble?

I will start with the Americans' ideas about tribalism. Initially, the occupation in Iraq was administered by the U.S. military. This was a role that the military did not want and indeed resented having to take on. That the generals were not prepared for this is evident from the conduct of the supreme commander, General Franks. Immediately after the war was over he ordered his commanders to prepare to draw down their forces. Within 30 days Franks wanted the total complement of U.S. troops in Iraq not to exceed 30,000.[3]

What changed General Franks's thinking was the anarchy which developed soon after victory was declared. Iraq was so engulfed by mayhem, of every variety; it would have been impossible for a small, residual force to have stayed on; it would have been massacred by the raging Iraqis.

So it was that the commanders of Franks's force had to hie themselves to the countryside to try to calm the populace. It is by observing their conduct in the process of going about seeking to accomplish this that we gain insight into what was in the Americans' minds, and consequently we can come to understand how benighted they were.

For example, in those early days the commanders reached out to the tribal chiefs. They evidently were taught—in their indoctrination sessions—that the chiefs were a power in Iraq, and that, with the Ba'th gone, they formed a loose network of control.

This was wrong. The tribal system remained strong in the Kurdish north but it certainly was not so in the South. There, successive republican regimes had succeeded in undercutting the old tribal connection. By the time that the Ba'th came along it was practically defunct. The British had severely weakened it and before them the Ottomans had degraded the system for their purposes of gaining control.[4]

Probably the biggest check to tribal authority was administered by the Ba'thists' successful carrying through of the land reform. Stripped of their hold over property, the tribal sheikhs suffered a significant diminution of power.

To be sure, tribal affiliation continued to count. However, it was nothing compared to the strength of the party. And over the course of the Iran-Iraq War (as I indicated in the last chapter), the party's power position had eroded as Hussein aggregated more and more power into his own hands.[5] Power in Iraq was *the* most centralized of any regime in the Middle East. It radiated from the Presidential Palace, to be wielded in the countryside by functionaries. Power in Basrah, or in Mosul or Arbil was the purview of appointed governors, and if a tribal leader wanted anything done, he went to him.

Hussein pursued a policy of continually undermining the tribal authority, and this effort—although reversed at intervals (when the president found it expedient to cultivate the sheikhs)—overall was a success. As a consequence, the Americans were rudely surprised when they appealed to the sheikhs for assistance running the country and the sheikhs begged off, excusing themselves on grounds they did not have the authority the Americans assumed.[6] The sheikhs retained the title, but little of real authority went with it.

One point that Americans too easily overlook in thinking about Iraqi society is that the Ba'th had been in power there for generations. Over the years, Iraqis had been brought around to the Ba'thist way not just of operating but of thinking. In the schools, tribalism was deprecated; the Bathists looked on it as retrogressive. Under a totalitarian form of rule (which certainly describes the Ba'th) it was not that difficult to change the way people thought. Especially when, as was the condition in Iraq, everybody spied on his/her neighbors.[7]

Moving from claims about tribalism, we turn next to the Americans views on sectarianism. Even before they had declared victory in Iraq they had arranged to anoint a spiritual leader of the Iraqi Shia community. (I will go into this in the next chapter.) They did this because they assumed that in Iraq the clergy was both respected and influential. With the Ba'th party gone, they expected to deal with the Shias through the ayatollahs.

Here again, as with their views about tribalism, the Americans were misinformed. The notion of Iraqis being totally devoted to their faith was overdone. Indeed after years of living under the Ba'th, an avowedly secular organization, the Iraqi Shias had no great concern for religion.

Just as the Americans believed that sectarian identity was important for Iraqis, so they believed the individual sects were rivalrous; that Sunnis mistrusted Shias, and Arabs Kurds, and so on. Indeed it was their belief that sectarian rivalry was only kept in check by the Ba'th. They believed that the party was a primarily Sunni organization, set up to look out for that community's interests; that it was not truly a national party—Shias and Kurds being virtually excluded from having a role in party life.

The Ba'th was not a Sunni party.[8] It was that at intervals, but under Hussein's leadership it swung back and forth, sometimes appealing to the Sunnis, at others to the Shias (it even sporadically would reach out to the Kurds). When Hussein took over the leadership in 1979, I said in the last chapter, a number of old-line Ba'thists conceived of it as a vanguard, much in the Leninist, Bolshevik tradition. These people, as I said, Hussein purged, and he did this at least in part to convert the party into a mass movement. To bring about this change he had to co-opt everyone that he could, without concern for sectarian ties.

As for the greater canard that the Sunnis shut the Shias out of government, this was a feature of Iraqi life *long before* the Ba'thists took over. The Shia sect deprecates temporal authority, the religious authority being the only one that counts.[9] As far back as the 1920s (when Britain entered the country), the ayatollahs forbade Iraqi Shias from taking part in public life,[10] a way of delegitimizing the regime.

Since no such prohibition obtained with the Sunnis, they flocked to government service. Much is made in the West of the Tikritis' privileged position in Iraq. (Hussein was from Tikrit, and it was Sunni.) But the Tikritis achieved their standing under the Hashemites. A Tikriti was head of the police, and, as would be expected in a society like that of Iraq, he filled the ranks with relatives.[11] When Hussein, aiming through repression to dominate Iraq, turned to the Mukhabarat, making it into his instrument of control, the Tikritis already were installed therein. Some of these people, however, were actual holdovers from the *ancien regime,* and the proteges that they had installed were, one must assume, their kinsmen.

This brings me to another matter overlooked by critics of the Ba'th: before the party came to power, all of southern Iraq, practically speaking, was the sphere of Iran. An anecdote about Hussein relates how, in the early 1970s, he visited Basrah, the leading city of the South (and almost 100 percent Shia) where the merchants refused to converse with him in Arabic, wanting him to come over into Farsi. Hussein responded by laying down the law: the southerners either accepted Iraqi citizenship, renouncing their Iranian tie, or they could leave, and many did leave.[12] However, a large part of that exodus was voluntary.[13]

Iranian hegemony over the South dated from before the period of the Shah, but the Shah worked hard during his reign to solidify his control. Iraq only came into existence as a state in 1932, and because for so many years— until the coming of the Ba'th—it was ruled by weak governments, Baghdad was never able fully to establish its authority in the South. Indeed the Iranian consul-general in Basrah was the de facto head of the area. If one wanted favors, he was the go-to person.[14]

That state of affairs was upset by two developments. First the Shah and Hussein composed their quarrel in 1975, which meant that Iran had to retreat on that front. But even before that, Iranian control over the Iraqi Shias had been weakened by the Shah's own crackdown on the religious leaders in his country. He did this in 1963 when he drove Khomeini out of the country. The combination of the two developments restricted the Iraqi's Shias from having contacts with their co-religionists next door.

When Hussein moved against the clerics, he did it not because he viscerally despised Shias, or more specifically Shia clerics, but rather because the ayatollahs were interfering with politics in Iraq. It was the case that Iraq under the Ba'th faced not one but two centers of subversion—the Shah's Fifth Column (which as I say effectively went out of business in 1975)[15] and the Iraqi Shia clerical establishment. However, since the clerics on both sides of the border despised temporal authority, the Iraqi contingent continued to reject the Ba'th. As long as the holiest sites in Shiadom—Najaf and Karbala—were located in Iraq, the ayatollahs regarded that part of the country as their appanage, viewing as an abomination secular Ba'thists' attempts to dictate affairs in the South.

Whatever the clerics may have believed, they exerted scant influence over the laity. Evidence of this is the high rate of intermarriage among the sects. Shias and Sunnis intermarried—until the Americans came no such aversion existed.[16] They also lived side by side in the cities. Only recently have Iraqis begun to withdraw into sectarian ghettos, driven to it by the breakdown of government authority in Iraq.

Finally, I want to discuss the record of the Shias in the Iran-Iraq War. If the Shias were so repressed why then did they fight in the Iran-Iraq War (the army, as I have already said, being 65 percent Shia)?[17] I have heard Americans claim that the Mukhabarat drove them to it. This is naïve, as I indicated in the last chapter.

I have noted that, at the outset of the Iran-Iraq War, rank-and-file Shias were not trusted by the Ba'thists, who feared they would go over to their co-religionists in Iran. But that attitude changed over the course of the war. By the end of it, Shias held commissions up to the level of corps commander—that is a lot of responsibility to entrust to one in whom you have no confidence.[18]

The Ba'thists always displayed willingness to trim their sails; to change course when circumstances warranted. During the Iran-Iraq War, the RCC, Iraq's ruling body, comprised 11 individuals, all top Ba'thists. In 1982, Hussein ordered a number of these to stand down, and in their place he appointed seven so-called presidential counselors—six of whom were Shias.[19] This gave the Shias a majority voice in running the country's affairs.[20] Nor were the top Shias mere tokens—one was the interior minister, which in Arab lands is a position of great power.[21]

The Americans, I think, were misled into believing that the sects were rivalrous. This was the view of expatriates like Chalabi and Makiya, both of whom had fled Iraq years before. In advising the Americans as to what were the conditions of life in Iraq, they drew on memories of the olden days, a way of life they were avid to see return. However, the Iraqis who remained in Iraq had no such yearning. That way of life, for them, was dead and gone. In the old days, society in Iraq was class ridden. Why want to see a return of that?[22]

Something else diminished the power of the religious: the cutoff of Shia pilgrimages. Pilgrimages to Najaf and Karbala were yearly rituals bringing considerable revenue to the South.[23] They were cut off during the Iran-Iraq

War for obvious reasons: most of the visitors came from Iran, and the Ba'th did not want saboteurs entering Iraq under the guise of performing the rite.[24] This cutoff imposed hardship on the community since it restricted trade. However, the Ba'thists were able to mitigate it by keeping up their guns-and-butter policy, funded by subventions from the Gulf sheikhs.

In any event, from what I saw in Iraq in 1984 (on my second visit there), I would say that assertive religiosity did not exist. No one in Iraq, that I saw, wore a beard, a sure sign of observance in the Middle East.[25] And certainly, there many fewer burkhas than now.

I said above that Khomeini's attempt to co-opt the Iraqi Shias stoked latent hostility between him and Hussein, ultimately leading to war. His agent in this was Ayotollah Mohammad Bakr al Sadr, the uncle of Moktada al Sadr, who presently is leading a section of the anti-American revolt. Khomeini met the elder Sadr when the Iranian leader took refuge in Najaf during the 1960s, a time when the Shah persecuted the Shia clergy at home. Iraq gave Khomeini shelter because the Shah was then an enemy of the Ba'th. When Hussein and the Shah composed their quarrel (in 1975) the Shah stipulated that Hussein expel Khomeini, which he did. (Khomeini went to Paris, whence he carried on his anti-Shah campaign.)

After the Shah was overthrown and Khomeini took power, Sadr proposed quitting Iraq, which by then had become too hot for him.[26] Khomeini, installed in Tehran, advised him to stay on, even though Hussein had threatened his life unless he left. And when Sadr complied with Khomeini's request and continued agitating (which meant taking the side of Iran against Iraq), Hussein had him executed.[27]

To some, the execution was a great injustice. I am sure it was, but *he was* warned. By continuing his attempts to undermine the government, Sadr provoked reprisal. And that step was not taken until his followers attempted to assassinate Ba'thists, among them the vice president, Tariq Aziz (who escaped, after a bomb was dropped on him).[28]

This rash of terrorist actions, carried out by Sadr's people, provoked the aforementioned crackdown by Hussein, which had the effect of driving a further exodus. Many religiously motivated Shias departed Iraq in those years, among them the Hakim brothers (more about them below). The departure cancelled citizenship. Sadr did not leave, hence he and his family remained Iraqis, while the Hakims became Iranians, de facto and de jure.

Something else worth knowing about the Iraqi Shias—*a good percentage were late converts to the faith*. They did not come on board, so to speak, until the 19th century, and then their reasons for converting, one could say, were mercenary.[29] The holy cities of Najaf and Karbala were sumptuously endowed by Shias from the Indian subcontinent, and under the terms of the endowment Shias living therein could claim support payments. The bedouin tribes, originally Sunni (at least nominally so), flooded into Najaf and Karbala where they converted more or less en masse. To this day, Iranian Shias look on their Iraqi co-religionists as less than firm adherents of the faith.

One can say that the rule in Iraq, in the lead-up to the Iran-Iraq War, was harsh: it was not a place where civil rights were respected. However, to claim that Hussein carried out a systematic repression of Shias (because they were Shias) is simply not tenable. Hussein's vision of Iraq, of what it could become, was ambitious: he not only sought to meld the separate communities into one, he wanted Iraq to be a thoroughly modern state, one that could compete with the industrialized west.[30] To accomplish this he had to utilize every human resource; he could not have risked a policy of deliberately alienating Shias—the majority group in the country.

Similar considerations operated in regard to the Ba'thists' attitudes towards women: women, under the Ba'th, were more highly regarded than anywhere in the Arab world: they held posts in government; served in various professional capacities, and in general their talents were recognized. Why? Because the Ba'thists needed their brain power.[31]

There, I will leave off discussing sectarianism to consider American misconceptions about the Kurds. The Americans believe that, during the Iran-Iraq War, the Kurds backed Iran. They did not. They were nominally allied with the Ba'th. To be sure, there was a persistent revolt carried on in the North of Iraq throughout the war. But that never involved more than a few thousand individuals, most allied in one capacity or another with the Barzani tribe.

The role of the Barzanis in Iraq, and their suppositious espousal of Kurdish nationalism, needs to be put in context. Effectively, the old chief, Mulla Mustafa, wore two hats. He was on the one hand the chief of his tribe, but he also assumed leadership of the so-called Kurdish Democratic Party (KDP). The party was the standard bearer of Kurdish nationalism in Iraq. Barzani was led to assume the leadership in the days of Qasem, when the Sole Leader required allies against the Arab nationalists; that is, the pro-Nasser faction.

In 1961 Qasem and Barzani fell out, and Barzani began his revolt which carried on intermittently up until 1975; then, with the first Iraq War, it leapt to life again. The Americans set up a no-fly zone over northern Iraq in the aftermath of that war, which allowed the Barzanis to establish themselves and win converts (more on that later).

I question whether Barzani was a sincere nationalist, or rather was bent on setting up as the principal warlord in the North, in which case he used nationalism as a vehicle for expanding his influence there.[32] The Americans believe that the Barzanis are the natural leaders of the Iraqi Kurds. In fact, many of the larger, older tribes disdain them. The tribe appeared relatively late (in the 19th century) and was formed by a self proclaimed religious leader. From its founding, the Barzanis had to fight against older established tribes, which more than once drove them into exile.

The Barzanis over the years operated as mercenaries. For example, in the 1940s, after being driven out of the North, they hired out as a protective force for the newly created Kurdish Republic of Mahabad, in Iran. When the Shah crushed that republic, the Barzanis fled to Russia where they remained for 13 years, returning when Qasem took over in Iraq. In a way, then, the tribe can be viewed as a mercenary army, letting itself out for hire—or at least this was the situation until comparatively recently.

My original assignment from the *Milwaukee Journal,* along with reporting on the Barzani revolt, was to investigate this suppositious movement of nationalism among the Kurds. I spent several weeks in the North of Iraq and confess I was hard put to find many proofs of strong national feeling there.

In those days the Kurds who were nationalists agitated for the creation of an autonomous zone. This was to exist within the confines of the Iraqi state. The autonomy idea was not a simple one, and the Kurds I interviewed seemed unable to conceptualize it. (Discussing the subject was difficult, because few Kurds I encountered spoke English, and so I had to work through interpreters, not all of whom were good.[33])

The fact of the revolt's being so ill defined, troubled me; however, that did not stop me from writing a series of articles which took the conventional view: that the Kurds were victims (of the Arabs); that their desire for a separate homeland was genuine, and so on. After years of intelligence work, much of it spent following the Kurds' career, I have changed my thinking. Two factors operate to determine conditions in the North of Iraq: one economic, the other cultural. From a cultural aspect, Kurdish society is more traditional than that in the South. I noted earlier that the Kurdish chiefs—so-called aghas—had successfully blocked introduction of reforms instituted among the Arab Iraqis.

What worked in the chiefs' favor was the geographic remoteness and inaccessibility of the Kurdish region. Much of Iraq is flat, until you come to the Kurdish north and then mountains rise precipitously achieving elevations of 3,000 feet. Such terrain encourages, or at least preserves, the institutions of tribalism; in that respect it most resembles Afghanistan. Tribes do not usually cooperate with each other. To be sure there are tribal confederations, but they form in times of crisis. Otherwise, the attitude of tribalists is one of mutual suspicion, if not outright rivalry.

The other, economic factor, is perhaps more interesting. For centuries the Kurds have pursued a vocation as smugglers. Smugglers want nothing to do with central government authority. If you are trafficking in contraband, your natural foe is the government, which wants its share of revenue in the form of taxes.

So it would appear that being autonomous, for the Kurds, translated into being left alone to get on with their smuggling. As for having a state of their own, why would they want such? They are much happier going their separate ways. I do not think anyone possibly could impute a desire for statehood to the Afghans. For any society built on illicit activity (with the Afghans, cultivating opium poppies), central government of any kind is anathema.

Nonetheless the belief is firmly held in the United States that the Kurds are ripe for self-determination. (And ironically, it is just as firmly believed that the Arab Iraqis are incapable of ruling themselves.) Indeed Kurdish nationalism is a staple of liberal opinion in the West. The *New York Times* is a strong advocate; it always has been. The newspaper sent out the first American reporter to cover the Barzani revolt. This was in 1963, with Dana Adams Schmidt.

William Safire, a contributing editor of the *New York Times,* was a champion of the cause, as were any number of other journalists. And, of course, the Israelis are very desirous of seeing a separate Kurdish state emerge (more on that below).

There is one more factor that impinges on the Kurds' role in Iraq, and that is oil. One of the richest oil fields in the world sits on the edge of the northern Kurdish territory: this is Kirkuk. When Hussein encouraged Arabs to immigrate to Kirkuk, this was a way of ensuring government control over the field.[34] Conversely, the Kurds have consistently held that Kirkuk is Kurdish and ought to be part of their territory.

Over the years, as the Barzanis and Iraqis sought to settle the Barzani revolt, the sticking point was this matter of who would control Kirkuk. Baghdad would not surrender it, yet the Barzanis year after year kept insisting on this.

In fact, the obdurateness of the Barzanis served the interests of Big Oil. I discussed in the last chapter how a succession of republican regimes tried to carry through on the oil nationalization. Obviously the oil interests were not desirous of seeing the republicans consolidate their rule, as that would facilitate the takeover. By stoking the revolt of the Barzanis, the interests embarrassed the republicans and drained national energies and resources which better could be expended building up the state.[35]

So the Barzanis' insistence on gaining control of Kirkuk is not so inexplicable, inasmuch as it served to keep the rebellion alive, and that served the oil interests—or it did until 1975, when Hussein and the Shah cut a deal whereby the Shah agreed to withdraw aid to the Kurds if Hussein would surrender half the Shatt al Arab.

That deal finished the Barzani revolt. Barzani was driven out of Iraq with his followers to seek asylum in Iran. (Subsequently, he died in Walter Reed Hospital in Washington.) But the tribe, the Barzani tribe, remained in residence in Iran, even after the Shah was overthrown, because Barzani's sons, Massoud and Idris, pledged fealty to Khomeini. When relations between the Islamic Republic and the Ba'th deteriorated (as they did under Khomeini) part of the problem was the Kurds. The Barzanis had returned to the North to stir up revolt there, at the instigation of the Khomeiniists.

The mass of Kurds, however, never got involved with this. They did not because Hussein bought them off.[36] Throughout all of the Iran-Iraq War, although the Barzanis managed to keep up a smouldering rebellion in the North, the Kurdish aghas kept faith with Baghdad, which meant that the whole of the Kurdish population backed the Ba'th—not out of love, but because Hussein had bought their loyalty.

The reader is going to ask, What about the infamous gassing of the Kurds, the so-called Anfal campaign, in which the Iraqis are supposed to have perpetrated genocide against them? The trials of the Ba'thists, wherein facts relating to the alleged genocide are supposed to be brought out, is still going on, and so there is not much I can say about this. This much I will say, however: I do not believe the Anfal ever happened. The reason I feel so is the following. The claims of how many Kurds are supposed to have been killed by gas are incredible. For the Iraqis to have killed 187,000 is simply impossible, because, as I have already indicated, gas is not a weapon of mass destruction.[37] Until someone can explain to me how so many could have died as a result of their being exposed to a weapon which has no such lethality, I will go on believing, as I do, that the Anfal is a hoax.[38]

Effectively, then, what can one say about the Americans' attitudes towards the Shias and Kurds (the two communities mainly of concern to them)? As to the Kurds, I would say that the Americans misconstrued the nature of that society. They regarded it as a society which would, had it not been thwarted by the Arab Iraqis, have evolved into an independent nation/state. They ought to have seen it more closely resembled Afghanistan: a tribal society, rent with all of the divisions which come into play with such a setup.

As for the Shias, there, the Americans were completely at sea, although they were not at all aware of this. The paradigm to which they related was seriously out-of-date. It had ceased to have relevance half way through the Iran-Iraq War. And I would argue that the reason it was never updated was because of influence of the neo-cons. It suited the neo-cons to believe that Iraq's Shias were disaffected from their government; that they were sworn enemies of the Sunnis, and that they were a priest-ridden community. After all, from the 1990s, the neo-cons, as we know, were maneuvering to get the United States into a war with Iraq. After 9/11 that activity went into high gear, as the neo-cons recognized, correctly, that Iraq could be implicated in the attack—not convincingly, to anyone who had any real knowledge of the country, but then few in the Washington policy making establishment could claim such knowledge.[39]

If Iraq was not a coherent entity, if the majority of Iraqis—Shias and Kurds—were alienated from the leadership of the Ba'th, then where was the harm in invading it? The invasion would be cost free, since there would be no defense put up by these two communities.

Something else operated to foul the intelligence-gathering effort just prior to the war. The neo-cons had cast the Iraqis as accomplices of Al Qaeda, and under the lash of Cheney and his people, the intelligence gatherers were being asked (nay, they were being compelled!) to find evidence of terrorist links. Thus all of the CIA's efforts, and of the Defense Intelligence Agency (DIA) and the State Department, were redirected to this futile search.

When the war was definitely embarked upon, effective intelligence gathering still was precluded, as the Defense Department under Wolfowitz's guidance, and with Douglas Feith in charge, kept the pressure on analysts to find evidence, not just of Al Qaeda-Iraq links but also that Iraq had WMD.

Thus the Americans went to war without any useful intelligence: they had a lot of half-baked ideas of Iraq the way it used to be and no longer was; ideas fed by Chalabi and Makiya (and also, interestingly, Bernard Lewis, who one would have thought would have steered clear of this).

One can understand the neo-cons behaving this way—*but the military?* It is inexcusable that America's military leaders would not have been better informed. For example, they disdained the Iraqi general staff. I recall partici- pating in a war game, before the war came off, and listening to a top U.S. general run down the Iraqis, insisting they were cowards and would not fight—did not know how to fight—their generals were so inept. This same general subsequently appeared practically nightly on television, counselling on how to fight the war, which by then was not going well—because the Iraqis were fighting.

Napoleon, in his *Maxims,* says that the most difficult thing for an army is to switch from defense to the offense, which, of course, is what the Iraqis succeeded in doing at the end of the Iran-Iraq War. Had the Americans cognized this, they might have been better prepared to counter the outside- in strategy switch the Iraqis employed in 2003, instead of being caught off guard as they were, which temporarily stalled the invasion.

To be sure, the Americans were influenced by the dismal performance of the Iraqis in the first Iraq War, where they tried to fight conventionally. However, there were reasons for the Iraqis' dismal showing in that war.[40]

So in any case, the war came off, and surprises came thick and fast for the Americans. The Iraqi regular army units, which the neo-cons insisted would not fight—because, being Shia, they were alienated from the regime—fought right down to the wire. And those Shia communities in the South which were expected to revolt against the Ba'th; to turn on and lynch the Ba'thists, fought alongside the units, seeking to repel the attack. Which provoked General Wallace's plaint: "This is not the war we wargamed for."

But the fiasco did not end there. Immediately after the Americans had declared victory, all available intelligence resources were dedicated to finding WMD. No effort was made to collect against the society; to try to develop sources from within the community. It was only later, when it was too late, that the Americans awoke to the realization that the moment when they might have recouped was gone. The Iraqis, having been thoroughly disaffected by the Americans' maladroitness in administering the occupation, had all (except the Kurds) turned against them; many, we must assume, having joined the resistance.

But the biggest error was made by L. Paul Bremer III, America's proconsul in Iraq, when he decided to cashier the Iraqi army officers and to disband the force. Bremer obviously believed the myth of the army being under the thumb of the party. With the party in disarray and Hussein in hiding, Bremer did not see that the army constituted a threat. Now leaderless, lacking direction, the army had self destructed, Bremer felt.

The Iraqi army had existed as a force-in-being for over 24 years. During that time it had fought three wars. In each its competency had improved, its professionalism had become more and more marked. It was now what it had never been before: an autonomous institution.

It did not matter if Hussein was in hiding, the Ba'th destroyed, the army was perfectly capable of acting on its own. Indeed all that was needed to galvanize it into action was an affront, one so grievous the officers would not countenance it, under any circumstances.

In signing his decree to disband the army, Bremer consigned it to the junk heap of history. The traditions of the corps, its pride in its accomplishments: the victories it had scored against Iran, all of this was as if it had never been.

Was the corps to accept this? Obviously no.

On May 24, 2003, 50 of the now cashiered officers, in a show of bravado, marched to the Presidential Palace where Bremer made his headquarters, and warned, he either rescinded his order or they would make him rue the day. "If they don't pay us, we'll start problems," said one 25-year veteran. "We have guns at home. If they don't pay us, if they make our children suffer, they'll hear from us."[41]

Bremer spurned the ultimatum.

The start of the Iraqi resistance can be dated to this confrontation. Nonetheless as attacks on Americans proliferated President George Bush insisted that they were random. It suited the administration to regard them as such because otherwise Bush would have had to admit that the mission was not accomplished; the war went on.

Shortly after Bremer issued his order, American officers serving in Iraq began to note, publicly, that a lot of the attacks showed a high degree of professionalism, appearing to indicate they were directed by military men—in other words, the ex-officers.[42]

Subsequently, the head of the Central Command, the effective director of operations in Iraq, General John Abizaid, told reporters the Americans were having to confront a "classical guerrilla-type campaign";[43] this followed a statement of the chairman of the Joint Chiefs, General Richard Meyers, to the effect that the military was "reassessing" its view of the resistance, to see whether it was "becoming better organized."[44] Up to this point,

Rumsfeld had been insisting (and indeed he went on doing so for some time) that the resistance was not serious, inasmuch (he said) as it was sporadic and disorganized.[45]

The resisters would lay clever ambushes where they would signal the approach of American armored columns by firing various colored flares. Those lying in wait would allow elements of the column to pass, then spring their trap, assaulting the Americans with small arms and rocket fire; then they would retreat into the countryside.[46] The insurgents would contest strategic roadways. The airport road in Baghdad, over which the Americans must pass to enter and leave the country, became a danger zone. So effective were the interdictions, passage to-and-from the airport became a lottery: no one who started on the road could say if he would arrive safely at his destination.[47]

There were other signs of a controlling hand behind the attacks. I noted in Chapter 1 widespread looting occurred once the American victory was declared. Now, attacks on government facilities continued, but it seemed loot was not the objective. The attackers gutted government ministries, trashing data banks so the offices could not function; then they would depart, *taking nothing with them.*[48]

June 2003 saw the first attack on the oil facilities, which patently was a strategic operation. Moreover, in carrying out their depredations, the attackers showed inside knowledge of how the facilities operated: they would attack crucial hookups, damaging them so not only was the oil flow interrupted, but also it could not easily be brought on line again.[49]

Attacks were made against the water system—*criminal elements do not try to shut off the country's water supply, or, for that matter, sabotage the electric grid, which was something else that occurred.*[50]

The insurgents regularly would shift their tactics, apparently with the aim of keeping the Americans off balance. Now they would focus on disrupting the government's operations; they would seek to interdict communications between strategic locales; they would sabotage the oil facilities. Former CIA officer, Milt Beardon, who had run a successful campaign of guerrilla warfare in Afghanistan, had this to say:

> The Americans and the British forces are facing a resourceful adversary whose game plan may be more developed than originally thought.
>
> To misread these attacks as desperation is dangerous. In the last two weeks, there have been multiple attacks on the Coalition headquarters in Baghdad, with mortars and rockets landing inside the secure Green Zone. Shoulder fired missiles have brought down a Chinook helicopter, killing 16 soldiers. The crash of a Blackhawk helicopter, killing an additional six, is still under investigation, but according to some reports, a rocket-propelled grenade may have brought it down. One or two casualties are logged almost daily.
>
> Ordinary criminals and thugs could not deliver this kind of punch. Mortar tubes, base plates and ammunition have to be smuggled within a few thousand

yards of the Green Zone, carefully set up and then launched in a shoot-and-scoot attack with timed delay.[51]

Now very much on the defensive, the Bush administration continued to maintain that this was *not* a popular resistance. It sought to downplay events, insisting that they were being brought under control. Then the first of the improvised explosive devices (IED's) appeared. Bombs were concealed in blocks of concrete, discarded oil cans; there was even a bomb packed into a lamppost.[52] Passing motorized columns of Americans would be shattered as the bombs were detonated remotely. The thin-skinned Humvees particularly were vulnerable. The Americans sought to counter the tactic, but as quickly as they did, the resisters would trump them. The fight against roadside bombs turned into a leapfrogging match: the Americans would figure out ways to neutralize the bombers, but then the bombers would change their *modus operandi*.[53]

For example, it was not long before the insurgents had adopted the so-called shaped charge which concentrates the bomb's blast, enabling it more effectively to penetrate armored vehicles. Another change the Americans noted was detonation by infrared lasers, an innovation aimed at bypassing electric jammers used to block radio-wave detonators.[54]

The really horrid development, however, was the tactic of suicide bombing. Starting in August 2003, a series of major attacks occurred in which car and truck bombs were used, where the drivers would incinerate themselves, a la Hizbollah against the U.S. Marine Corps barracks in Lebanon in 1983. First, the Jordanian embassy in Baghdad was hit on August 7, 2003 (11 people were killed)[55]; next came the UN headquarters in Baghdad, demolished in a huge blast on August 19th, killing 20—including the UN secretary general's special representative, Sergio Viera de Mello[56]; on August 29, 95 worshipers perished in an attack on a Shia shrine in Baghdad, which also killed Muhammad Bakr al Hakim, the head of the Iranian-sponsored SCIRI (more on him below)[57]; on October 12, a bomb went off outside a Baghdad hotel used by Americans, killing 35[58]; two weeks later, while Wolfowitz was staying at the same hotel, it was rocketed[59]; and finally on November 12 at least 26 Italians and 9 Iraqis were killed and 195 people injured when the Italian compound was struck in Nasiriyah.[60]

The reaction worldwide was one of horror, because of the high toll in civilians. However, by targeting non-American installations (such as the Italian compound), and causing death and destruction among foreign forces serving in Iraq, the attacks had an unwelcome (for the Americans) effect: the Bush administration was lobbying foreign governments to send troops to Iraq; not only did that support not materialize, but also some foreign forces already in-country were withdrawn. Evidently their governments judged it too dangerous to stay on.[61]

At the same time the appearance of suicide bombers gave the administration an opportunity to turn the tables—or so it seemed. Bush proclaimed that the bombers were Muslim fanatics (jihadis), slipping into Iraq from Syria to sabotage the country's march to democracy. In other words, the administration went from blaming the violence on Ba'thist "dead-enders" to claiming that it was a *jihad, run by foreigners.* Bush further came up with a name of an individual who supposedly was directing the effort, a so-called lieutenant of Osama bin Laden, one Abu Musab al Zarkawi. According to Bush, *Zarkawi was the mastermind of the revolt.*

In making its claims, the administration revealed its ignorance. It connected Zarkawai to Al Qaeda through an outfit called *Ansar al Islam.* This supposedly was Bin Laden's dog in the Iraq fight (if I can put it so).[62] Circumstances argue against this being the case. Ansar al Islam operated from a base flush up against the Iranian border, in the high mountain area of Kurdish Iraq. If it was there, it was there for a purpose: the guerrillas wanted to be able to duck over into Iran whenever hard pressed by foes on the Iraqi side.

Now, if Ansar al Islam was indeed an Iranian client (as I believe it would have to be, given where it was situated), *it could not have been allied with Al Qaeda,* a Wahhabi outfit—the Wahhabis and the Shias are deadly enemies. Indeed it is practically certain that Ansar al Islam was a latter-day version of an organization that existed during the Iran-Iraq War, an Islamic Kurdish group inserted into Iraq by the Iranians in 1983, to counter two other Iraqi Kurdish rebel groups, Barzani's outfit, the so-called Kurdish Democratic Party, and the Patriotic Union of Kurdistan (PUK) of Jelal Talabani. (I will have more to say about Talabani in the next chapter. Originally allied with Barzani, he split with him early on, and to this day the two men are rivals.)

To a nonspecialist reader, this matter of intriguing among rival guerrilla groups may be confusing; I will expand on it. When the Iran-Iraq War broke out, Syria confounded the rest of the Arab world by taking the part of the Islamic Republic against Iraq. Syria did this because its leader, Hafiz al Assad, bore a personal grudge against Saddam Hussein: they led rival wings of the Ba'th Party, but over and above this, Assad had never forgiven Hussein for refusing to ally Iraq with Syria in the anti-Israel fight (this goes back to events of 1979, when Hussein claimed to have uncovered a plot to bring Iraq into union with Syria). In any event, in 1983 the Iranians tried to invade Iraq through the Kurdish north, and Barzani's KDP guerrillas assisted that attempt.[63] Afterward, Barzani expected the Islamic Republic to turn over to him a tract of ground seized in the invasion. Instead Khomeini gifted it to a newly created outfit, the aforementioned SCIRI. This enraged Barzani and he, in a pet, went over to the side of Damascus. Assad was already patronizing Talabani. So now Assad had succeeded in co-opting the two relatively substantial Kurdish opposition groups away from Iran.

The Iranians, always jealous of Syrian attempts to extend their sway over Iraq, to make up for this loss created a new group, comprising Kurdish Shias.[64] For awhile during the Iran-Iraq War this outfit operated in the North, staking out its own territory, which it guarded against both the guerrillas of Barzani and Talabani. After the Iran-Iraq War, the Islamic Kurds continued in a client relationship with Iran, and consequently existed as a force-in-being. It would have been natural for them to reactivate themselves once the American invasion came off, since the two original Iraqi Kurdish rebel groups—the KDP and PUK—had gone over to the Americans.

The point of all this is that the Bush administration did not understand the enemy. It never did; it still does not. The argument for Zarkawai's being the mastermind of the revolt was further discredited when an essential bit of evidence, supposed to prove the Al Qaeda tie, was shown to be hyped. According to a report in the *Washington Post,* the U.S. Army, as part of a psyche-war operation, was promoting Zarkawi's group to be more effective—and more extensive—than it was. This, to deceive Americans, according to the *Post,* into believing the fighting in Iraq was religiously inspired, *by foreigners.*[65]

At any event, after promoting this theory, about fanatics slipping into Iraq, Bush ordered the U.S. Army to seal the border with Syria whence the jihadis supposedly were infiltrating. Large scale antiterrorist operations commenced in Iraq's far west Anbar province. Unfortunately (for the Americans) when the operations were over, the Army reported few, if any foreigners had been apprehended.[66]

That, however, was not the worst of it. For, in extending operations to the Syrian border area, the Americans stirred up a hornet's nest. As in the case of the Kurds, smuggling activity is rife in this part of Iraq; it always has been—*for decades.* Whole families, whole villages, *whole tribes* have traditionally made this their livelihood.[67] When the Americans went into the area, it was these smugglers that they had to confront. The smugglers were not about to let the Americans take over their area, any more than the Kurds had been willing to do with the Ba'thists. Suddenly, obscure villages—actual way stations on the smuggling route—became the focus of fierce fire fights.[68] The Americans, who had expected to move into the area and easily take charge there, were stunned by the intensity of the resistance encountered. The whole of western Anbar Province exploded.

Now we come to Fallujah.

Whatever produced this ugly incident, I do not think anyone knows. The event has assumed iconic significance: the grisly spectacle of American civilian contractors, their incinerated corpses dangling from ropes over the Euphrates, shocked the world. American public opinion was galvanized as it had not been since Somalia. It was seen—without possibility of denial—that some Iraqis did not like Americans; *indeed, they viscerally despised them.*

During the earlier invasion phase, American forces had stayed out of Fallujah. It was only afterward that the U.S. Army went in, and then it adopted a cautious, low-profile approach: it sought to keep out of people's way.[69] For as long as the U.S. Army remained in the area, nothing untoward occurred (although it was obvious the Fallujans were deeply mistrustful).

In March 2004, Marine units replaced the Army, and the new Marine command determined on a show of force.[70] On March 25, a convoy of Marines moving through Fallujah was hit by a homemade bomb and then attacked by insurgents. One Marine was killed and two wounded.[71] The following day the command sent a force of 300 Marines into the neighborhood where the attack had occurred. They were immediately fired on by Iraqis. In seeking to repel the attackers, the Marines killed 16 people and lost one of their own; also killed was an ABC television cameraman.

The ambush in which the contractors died came a week later, and like earlier attacks it showed every sign of having been orchestrated: reports noted the sophistication of the attackers, which would appear to indicate the officers were involved. Moreover, the attackers moved easily through the area. In fact they had the backing of the community, as later was demonstrated when Fallujah rose against the Americans. Iraqis barricaded themselves in quarters of the city to which Americans were denied entry. Overnight, Fallujah became enemy territory; a no-go area.

It is what happened next that is so incomprehensible. At a time when it was clear that the Americans already were being challenged, Bremer decided they ought to go after the aforementioned Moktada al Sadr.[72] Moktada was a minor cleric, but scion of the Sadr family. His uncle and father, having been respected clerics, the Sadr name had great weight. Sadr's bailiwick was Sadr City, a huge, sprawling quarter of Baghdad (home to over a million Iraqis, mostly Shias). Sadr City has a history dating back to the founding of the republic. It was created by Qasem (he called it al Thawrah, the revolution). The quarter was then—and still is to this day—the home of Shias who originally constituted a destitute mass. Under the Hashemites, so-called *Shurugis* (easterners), individuals from depressed areas of the Shia south, gravitated to Baghdad in search of work. They created a giant shanty town on the outskirts of the capital. A British army doctor who toured there in the 1930s described the denizens as "pathological specimens" of practically every known disease.[73]

Under the Hashemites, no effort was made to improve the lot of these people, and, to a certain degree, this was the fault of upper class Shias, who disdained the Shurugis. Qasem, in an attempt to compensate them, built Al Thawrah; it became the Shurugis' new home (instead of tar paper shacks, they now had concrete blocks to live in). Al Thawrah was kept up under the Ba'th but the name changed to Saddam City, and after the Ba'thists fell it was rechristened Sadr City after Moktada's uncle, who had been executed by Hussein.

In any event, Bremer went after Sadr, for reasons he never made clear. It is my theory he was put up to it by the expatriates. These expatriates, as I intend to bring out in the next chapter, were a pernicious influence on the occupation. The expatriates were all non-Iraqis, even though they claimed to be bona fide citizens of the state of Iraq. And because they had developed strong ties to interests in the United States (most notably the neo-cons, and the conservative think tanks, like the American Enterprise Institute), they were able to cut quite a swath in Washington. Two of the expatriates were Shias, Ahmed Chalabi and Muhammad Bakr al Hakim, both of whom were angling to become the leader of the Iraqi Shia community. Moktada, who had remained in Iraq and never fled, as had these two, was their natural rival.

Bremer (for reasons I will make plain in the next chapter) had been increasingly led to cooperate with the expatriates and, I believe, either one or the other of the expatriates, or perhaps both, induced him to go after Sadr. Something else comes into play here. Although anti-American, Moktada also opposes Iran; he does not want to see Iraq annexed by the Islamic Republic, an outcome the expatriates were trying to effect.

Bremer's excuse, the excuse he gave for so acting, was that Sadr had killed another ayotollah, Abdul Majid Khoi, whose killing I will discuss in the next chapter. This Khoi assassination was an extremely murky business. No one knows who did the job, and in terms of who stood to benefit from Khoi's death, it was the Iranians.

In any event, Bremer out of the blue launched an attack on Sadr. Sadr immediately raised the standard of revolt. The response was extraordinary. A huge outpouring rallied to his cause. This turnout, as has been the case with much that has gone on in Iraq, was misinterpreted by the media. In the West it was treated as though Sadr always was a power in Iraq, and, as if his militia, the so-called Mahdi Army, always had existed.

However, this could not have been the case. The Ba'thists, as I pointed out above, were masters of surveillance, and also obsessed with keeping power exclusively in their hands. To be sure, the Ba'th had been under pressure in the period immediately leading up to the second Iraq War (because of the sanctions), but it never became so weakened and disoriented that it could not enforce discipline. Hence to assume that Sadr could have built a power base under the Ba'th is not tenable.

It has to have been the case that the Mahdi Army *did not exist* until Sadr called it forth. Which is to say that Sadr, an astute politician, saw that the Shias would welcome the opportunity to confront the occupiers, and thus he issued his call—a long shot that paid off. The youth—and it was mainly youth who responded—turned out en masse.

What was more astonishing is not just the Baghdadis of Sadr City reacted, the response was widespread—throughout the entire south! Are we to believe that Sadr had militiamen implanted in Najaf, Karbala, and even in

Basrah? When would he have put them there? To build an organization capable of operating underground (under the Ba'th), one which could then be called to action in a moment of crisis, would have been beyond his capability.

This rising of the Shias and the sudden appearance of a supposedly fully formed opposition group, the Mahdi Army, had to have been a spontaneous occurrence. The Shias were deprived of essential services, no jobs, constant insecurity. Things had grown so bad under the Americans that, in the eyes of the youth, they could hardly have been worse off.

At the same time, I do not think that Sadr conspired with the ex-army officers. I see no evidence of this. But what of it? If my theory is correct, that the rising of the Shias indicated widespread disaffection, then his action in calling for revolt, added to the officers already in arms, added up to something in the nature of a national rising.[74]

Indeed the outpouring was such that, momentarily, it stunned the Americans, and once it got going, it could not be brought back under control.

This highlights another failure of the Occupation Authority. The Americans maintained, prior to going into Iraq, that the Shias were the most important community there, but when it came to allotting areas of control, they assigned the Shia southlands to their coalition allies: the British, the Poles, and the Italians.

Why, if the Shias were so important, did the Americans not garrison the community themselves? To be sure, they were short on troops. Nonetheless, Najaf—the center of the Shia faith—at least ought to have been their lookout. As it was, the British, who were mainly responsible for the South, made a mess of it.

The British went into Iraq with an insufficient force (a mere 40,000) and so were hard put to maintain order. They availed themselves of help from—of all people—the Iranians! When the occupation was established, the South remained in a disturbed state, and in the ensuing turmoil, Iranians were enabled to slip over the border. These groups (for they were all well organized) were meant by the Iranians to constitute a Fifth Column, looking out for Tehran's interests in Iraq.

Two of the groups that entered in this way were the SCIRI party, about which I have already spoken, and the so-called Badr Brigades. The Brigades constituted SCIRI's milita.

The British foolishly agreed with a proposition put to them by the Iranians that they be allowed to assist in keeping control. This they would do by undertaking joint patrols. And the British accepted the arrangement!

What folly! For who after all were these Badr Brigade people? They were the same individuals of whom I spoke in Chapter 2, who had thrown down their arms in the early days of the war; capitulated in the face of the human wave attacks, and eventually turned their coats, going over to the side of the Islamic Republic. In other words, they were renegade Iraqis.

The *brigadistas* had been living outside Iraq since the early days of the Iran-Iraq War; however, they returned once in 1991 when the Iraqi Army was driven out of Kuwait. In the general confusion, the Brigades slipped back into Iraq, seeking to foment a revolt. That revolt failed to take hold; the Iraqi Shias did not respond, and Hussein's Republican Guard was able to put it down brutally. The beaten Brigades slunk back to Iran—what was left of them.

Now, thanks to the British, they were back, lording it over the Basrawis. Swanning around, showing themselves off, giving orders. The brigadistas behaved very much as had the Popular Army men in the early 1960s when that group asserted itself and in the process alienated the Arab officers.

The same reaction now developed with the Basrawis—they resented the appearance of these carpet baggers. I think it is likely the overwhelming response to Sadr's call to revolt was due to this; that is, to the southerners' displeasure at having to submit to the authority of individuals for whom they had no regard; indeed, whom they had every reason to despise.

The brigadistas tried to amend public behavior: they shut down liquor shops; they chastised women for appearing in public "shamelessly" dressed; they trashed brothels.[75] All this certainly upset the secular Iraqis, and I imagine it would have proved equally offensive to Iraqis generally.

What I am saying is that, just as the revolt of the ex-officers was provoked by Bremer, so this revolt too, of Moktada, was provoked. I do not believe that there would have been a revolt of the Shias had Bremer left Moktada alone, and had the British not compromised themselves by teaming up with the Brigades.

In any event I think now we can characterize the resistance: it started out as a patriotic response of Iraqis seeking to repel the American invasion; it then developed into a mutiny of the ex-officers, who felt they had a grievance against Bremer. I can find no evidence that the officers originally intended more than to gain restitution; I do not think they intended to foment a popular uprising. The Americans, making various wrong moves, did this for them. First off, the U.S. military drove the smugglers of Anbar to resist; then Fallujah became enflamed; and then Bremer, acting on what impulse I am sure I cannot explain, went after Moktada. Moktada's revolt comprised an enormous number of individuals (at least 60,000). But we must also be aware that the army, inasmuch as it comprised, at its height, a million men under arms, constituted practically a microcosm of Iraqi society. So this was not just two discrete groups in opposition—this represented a considerable portion of the Iraqi public in arms.

Bush could claim that the resistance was a conspiracy fomented by Al Qaeda. I doubt it strongly. To be sure, Al Qaeda may have been involved, but if it was, the part it played was a minor one. Basically this was a *native* revolt, one which originated from the bottom up—no one directs it from on high (as far as I can see). It is the repeated gaffes of the Occupation Authority that keep it going.

There is one other point I want to make before I end the chapter. What happened in Iraq during the April (2004) events is perhaps not as important as *what did not happen.* The Americans, in attempting to regain control, had practically to do the job themselves. All of the parties whom they had singled out for special favor in Iraq, that is, the collaborationists whom they raised to high positions in the newly formed government, *not one* was of help in the crisis.

Ayotollah Sistani, whom the Americans had anoited as spiritual guide of the Shias, hid out in his palace in Najaf, evidently waiting for the revolt to blow over. When the revolt waxed fiercer and fiercer, Sistani was driven to make a statement, but he merely deplored the violence, refusing to condemn Sadr.

The Badr Brigades became involved to be sure, but only because Sadr's people attacked them. The Mahdi Army fell on the brigadistas with a vengeance. And the Iranians did not acquit temselves well in this contest.

Ahmed Chalabi—even though he had his own militia, the so-called Iraqi National Accord—he too kept a low profile.

And Iyad Allawi, another Shia, who had just been elevated to prime minister under the occupation, after first adopting a tough stance of swearing to put the revolt down, retreated to the sidelines.

The Kurdish north remained peaceful, but as the Kurds did not venture out of the North, they were of little help to the Americans in quelling the unrest.

Bremer initially hung tough, ordering the Army and Marines to crack down: make American control a reality. The proconsul evidently believed that "a sputter of musketry," as Churchill so famously remarked, would serve as a corrective. He was wrong there. So widespread did the unrest become, an order for the withdrawal of a U.S. Army division had to be countermanded.[76] The division began rushing 70-ton battle tanks to Iraq from its home base in Germany.[77]

Additional reserves had to be called up; National Guard units in the United States were mobilized.[78] Nor was this a mere rattling of sabres. April was going down as the worst month for casualties since the start of the war. Since May 1, 2003, when Bush declared an end to major combat, 548 U.S. military personnel had been killed.[79]

Furthermore, there was not any letup. Daily, the *muezzens* would issue the call to arms. Everywhere were seen black bearded, beturbaned clerics striding through the neighborhoods, brandishing Klashnikovs, crying out and hand gesturing to the faithful to turn out; get down into the street; fight the Americans!

This visible presence of clerics taking an active role, confirmed to Bush that this was indeed jihad. He advertised it as *a clash of civilizations.* So here again, the Americans were claiming that fanatics were responsible. It was not a homegrown insurrection of native Iraqis (Bush said); it was a work of "outside agitators."

But events on the ground belied this. For one thing, there were numerous reported instances of Shias and Sunnis cooperating. Imams in their Friday prayer sermons exhorted their congregants to put aside sectarian differences and unite—Sunnis and Shias together against the Americans.[80]

Meanwhile in the West the press speculated that Iraq was slipping into civil war. I do not believe it, not at this stage. All of the groups—the ex-army officers, the smugglers of Anbar, the Fallujah natives and now Moktada's people—agreed on one thing: America out of Iraq! Also, and this is most interesting, they all opposed the expatriates, whom they viewed (correctly) as agents of Iran. Thus the revolt had a certain coherence.

What additionally I find extraordinary is the befuddled nature of the American response. It was bad enough they undertook the invasion and occupation of Iraq with inadequate knowledge of the country, but that they then would keep on making mistakes, based on ignorance, is mystifying.

The Americans might have seen that their government-formation scheme was not working; that in particular the expatriates, whom they had selected to run Iraq, were being shown up as ineffective. Had they come to that realization, they might then have reversed course and found another way forward. They could at least have reassessed what went on in the invasion phase, where they had encountered popular resistance in Nasiriyah, Najaf, Samawah, and Basrah. This would have tipped them to the fact that the popular support they had counted on, going into Iraq, was not there.

They did not do any of this—as we will see in the next chapter. I think now I have answered one of the main questions we needed to address; that is, why was the occupation so badly handled? It was a matter of bad intelligence. The Americans had no good intelligence going into Iraq, and once in they failed to develop reliable sources of information among the natives. They trusted to their preconceived notions of what Iraq was like—the delusions I referred to above. But their conception, as I tried to show, was shot full of contradictions, as even the most rudimentary reflection would have shown. The Americans refused to reflect, and hence, as we will see, they just kept going wrong.

4

Expatriates vs. Natives

The Bush administration evidently had a plan for how it was going to run Iraq after the war was over. It was, however, not very clearly defined or even for that matter well thought out. For example, Wolfowitz, before the invasion took place, had handpicked a team of Iraqi-Americans to go to Iraq and lay down the lines along which the new government would form (that is, once the war was won and the Ba'th toppled).[1] The individuals selected were a self-effacing, retiring lot. Few would give their names to the press, fearing, as they said, harm from the Iraqis. Several seemed to be banking on as short a stay as possible in-country, and one fellow went so far as to opine that he would like to do the task assigned him from Sweden.[2]

At the same time as to what precisely the team was charged with implementing; what plan it was operating under, nothing of that came out. All of the team members were technocrats so that might have given a clue as to the direction Wolfowitz's thoughts were tending.[3] But, then, if the administration was thinking *technocratically,* it picked a strange individual to put in charge of the delegation. The leader—and the neo-cons' favored candidate for running the new Iraq—was Ahmed Chalabi: anything but a bland technocrat he![4] Chalabi was a high flyer, a character adept at self promotion, but someone without many—*if any*—qualifications for carrying out civil affairs functions.[5] In interviews granted to the press before departing for Iraq, Chalabi set forth no plan of what he would do there, except to say (over and over) that he was going to purge the Ba'thists.[6] Chalabi seems to have conceived of himself as a Grand Inquisitor: he would create the institutions whereby the Occupation Authority could filter out Ba'thists seeking to gain entry into the work force.

Essentially, then, what Wolfowitz had cobbled together as a leadership team was a varied lot of individuals: some timorous seeming technocrats, behaving as though they regretted ever having gotten involved with the enterprise (so fearful were they of what might be lying in store for them in Baghdad); and one flamboyant character, namely, Chalabi; but he seems not to have any ideas other than to carry out a purge. There was not anything *positive* the Americans were setting forth to do, seemingly.

Oh, to be sure there was some additional activity going on inside Iraq. A few individuals whom the Americans had preselected to assume leadership roles had come forth.[7] But in line with this there was a shocking incident that occurred. The Americans had flown back into Iraq (from his exile home in London) one Ayatollah Abdul Majid Khoi. The fact of their having flown him in signified that he was *persona grata;* the Americans clearly had a role they intended him to play. However, Khoi was not in the country but a few days when he was hacked to death outside the main mosque in Najaf.[8] As to who his assassins were, a number of theories were put forth. It was hinted that Moktada might have done the deed, but then some other reports implicated another cleric, an actual ayatollah; this was Muhammad Bakr al Hakim. Hakim headed the Supreme Council of the Islamic Revolution in Iraq, which I mentioned in the last chapter.[9]

This nastiness of Khoi's being murdered and suspicion falling on members of the clerical establishment in Iraq plunged the Occupation Authority within days of its having begun operations into the murkiest of intrigues. One possible explanation of what (or who) was behind this follows.

Khoi subscribed to a doctrine within Shia Islam which enjoins clerics to stay out of politics. One can see how this would appeal to the Americans, who were, as they had revealed publicly, keen on setting up a form of rule ideally staffed with moderates. However, opposing this quietist school is another tendency, fabricated by the former Iranian leader, the late Ayatollah Ruhollah Khomeini, which contrarily takes the position that only clerics are fit to govern. And, of course, it is the Khomeini line that predominates in Iran—all of the leaders there are Khomeiniists. Since, as now seems certain, the Iranians were aiming from before the victory of the Americans to assert themselves in Iraq—with what specific intent at this stage was unknown— they would not have wanted a cleric tipped by the Americans as spiritual guide of the Iraqi Shias. So it might well have been the case that agents of Hakim murdered Khoi. (As for Moktada's supposititious complicity I do not know on what grounds he might have been.)

Hakim, as the Americans ought to have known, was an agent of Iran, sent to Iraq to carry on its machinations there. He had not been invited in by the Americans (as had Khoi). He just showed up, crossing into Iraq at Basrah not long after the victory was declared.[10] The Iran-Iraq border has always been porous; after the American invasion it became more so. Since, as I have pointed out already, the Americans invaded with insufficient force, they have not the means to police it adequately (to this day).[11]

At the same time Hakim had a basis for being in-country: he and his group, SCIRI, had been certified—in a manner of speaking—by no less a party than Martin Indyk, Bill Clinton's principal Middle East advisor at the State Department.[12] This was back in 1999, when Indyk handpicked seven expatriate Iraqis whom the United States felt it could support as an exile-opposition to the Ba'th. All of the others so selected might have been seen as defensible choices. Hakim and SCIRI were problematic. They may have suited in the late 1990s when America was reaching out to Tehran, hoping to steer it toward becoming a friend of Washington. But subsequently Bush had labeled Iran one of the "Axis of Evil" states. It did not make a lot of sense, now, for the Americans to allow so potentially disruptive a character as Hakim into the country, much less let him stay.

Further, after their initial visit to Washington (in 1999) Hakim and SCIRI never returned. There were some contacts evidently but most interestingly the SCIRI people never participated in any of the planning for the invasion as had all of the other expatriates (about which more in a minute).[13] The SCIRI people had not accepted funding from the United States, as had the others. One would have thought such behavior would have warned the Americans to be wary of this group.[14]

In regard to Hakim's unannounced (and unanticipated) appearance, the Americans raised no objection: they let him stay. Probably two considerations operated here. On the one hand, Hakim had come to Iraq with his own personal militia, the so-called Badr Brigades (discussed above). Having a lot of armed militiamen in Baghdad, a city descending into anarchy, had to have given pause to the Americans.[15] The U.S. military may have figured that to eject Hakim would raise a ruckus: not welcome, given the way things were going. Moreover, it was not as though the brigadistas were all together in one place, conveniently located in Baghdad (where they could be rounded up and dispatched): they were dispersed throughout the country, many having stopped off in Basrah, the preserve of the British.[16] It was these people whom the British, as I said in the last chapter, had decided to co-opt into policing the southland.

For the British, the arrangement seemed to work out well. At least they did not complain. However, the Brigade members were ultimately to cause considerable trouble for the Occupation Authority; immediately, however, the joint patrolling arrangement seemed to work.[17] It may be that Hakim made a similar offer to the Americans in Baghdad. I do not know. What I do know is that he offered to support American efforts to hold elections.[18] For reasons which will become clear, Iran was anxious to see the process of government formation get started, and succeed.

Whatever the reason, Hakim and the Badr Brigade were allowed to stay. A serious misjudgment on the Americans' part, I think.

At the same time, although the Americans were not about to eject Hakim, they evidently had no intention of taking him on as their client (as they seemed to have been planning to do with Khoi), and this is interesting because at the time they were on the lookout for a replacement for Khoi. With that individual gone, the Americans evidently figured they needed someone whom they could certify as spiritual head of Iraq's Shias.

This is in line with the Americans' perception that the Shias were primarily devoted to their religion, which I tried to show in the last chapter was old thinking. They were thoroughly secularized and as such would not have wanted a religious figure to be put over them.

Moreover, I am going to argue that, for purposes of controlling the country, this predisposition of the Americans to privilege the clergy was a mistake. As we will see, it makes for great problems for them, in a way that one would not expect.

There was also the fact of the Americans having Chalabi. He was a Shia, and so they could have set him up as a leader of the Shia community; the neo-cons certainly would have wanted that.[19] Chalabi was their boy, so to speak. A frequent speaker at the American Enterprise Institute, columnist in the *Wall Street Journal* and what all, Chalabi had for a number of years prior to the invasion been buttering up all the "right" people in Washington.

The original plan may have been for Chalabi to be the real, behind-the-scenes leader in Iraq, with Khoi, a figurehead, conferring a patent of religious authority on projects Chalabi laid on.

If that was the aim, the neo-cons' scheme ran into difficulty. Chalabi, as it turned out, was a loser[20]; the Iraqis did not like him. There were a number of reasons for this, the most notable being that he had fled the country in 1958 when the Hashemites were overthrown. That meant that, in Iraqi eyes, Chalabi was a monarchist, and I described in Chapter 2 how dreadfully the Iraqis treated the Hashemites when they deposed them. To invite a proponent of the monarchist form of government back to Iraq to play a prominent role in politics was not a good idea—something on the order of returning a Bourbon to France after 1789 or a Romonov to Russia after the Bolshevik Revolution. Nonetheless, a prominent neo-con, David Wurmser, was strong for returning the Hashemites to rule, and he evidently had set up an interview at the State Department for the scion of the dynasty, which was held just before the invasion.

Along with that, Chalabi, after leaving, never returned to Iraq—until 1991 when he slipped back into the northern Kurdish territory whence he ran what he described as several big anti-Ba'thist operations (all of which flopped). This sorjoin, from 1991, immediately after the first Iraq War and until the outbreak of the second Iraq War, was marked in the Kurdish area by an unusual situation. After the first Iraq War the Americans set up a no-fly zone over northern Iraq and warned the Ba'thists against sending military units there; so that part of the country effectively was severed from

Baghdad's control. This left it free for Masoud Barzani (of the KDP), and Jelal Talabani (of the PUK) to move in—along with Chalabi and some other expatriates—and take over there. In fact the Kurdish aghas were the ones really in charge, since, as had always been the case, they were the power in the North. But the aghas, a canny lot, saw the merit of cooperating with Barzani and Talabani. The two had the ear of the Americans and thus were in a position to dispense favors.

There seems to have been an exchange: Barzani and Talabani, neither of whom was held in very high regard by the aghas, were allowed by them to pose as leaders in the North; in return, the two steered various beneficences the aghas' way. In effect, Barzani and Talabani became self-constituted warlords, drawing enterprising Kurds into their entourages. Barzani set up in the far north, his father's old stamping ground. Talabani's headquarters was around Sulaymaniyah, an area that he knew well having once been the province's governor, a post conferred on him by Hussein.[21]

The Bush and Clinton administrations proclaimed Kurdistan, as they called it, a free, democratic entity from 1991 until 2003. It was not. No Kurd, who was not of agha status, dared cross Barzani and Talabani—anymore than anyone pre-2003 would have crossed Hussein.[22]

In any event, despite Chalabi's posturing—he went everywhere in Iraq and took part in all Occupation Authority activities—he failed singularly to make an impression on the Iraqis. U.S. military officers reported that working through him to get anything done was a waste of time; it was worse than useless—it was counterproductive.[23] It was enough for Chalabi to espouse a program, for the Iraqis to balk at implementing it.

Casting about for a replacement for Khoi—someone who was not Hakim—the Americans hit on one Ali Sistani.[24] He was, as had been the case with Khoi, an ayatollah. And unlike Chalabi (and Hakim, who had fled Iraq in 1982), Sistani had remained in-country throughout the Iran-Iraq War. He was also, like Khoi, a quietist, which probably was why the Ba'thists tolerated him: he kept out of politics.[25] Also of interest, Sistani was a notorious recluse. A septuagenarian, he rarely left his palace in Najf, and later, when the Americans came to deal with him, he refused to meet them personally; they had to negotiate through intermediaries.

It was not long before western journalists began referring to Sistani as "the most respected religious figure" in Iraq, which implied that Sistani was slated for co-optation, and it was hinted that, now, with him on board, things would move smartly under the occupation. This was pure speculation on the journalists' part. They assumed that Sistani, being an ayatollah—the equivalent of a cardinal—must be a figure much beloved by the Shias. Was he? We will see.

After Khoi's death, the next severe jolt that affected the Occupation Authority was the removal of General Garner.[26] Retired General Jay Garner had been tapped by Rumsfeld to be America's proconsul in Iraq. He had familiarity with Iraqis, having been the U.S. representative to the Kurds in the 1990s when they set up that free zone I just mentioned in the North.

Evidently the Americans did not look on Garner as a keeper. He probably was selected on short notice, to fill the slot. In any event, within months after he took up his assignment he was out. That Washington would make so great a change so unexpectedly (it took everyone by surprise) was odd. What was worse, the Americans had allowed Garner to put certain schemes into play, most notably the general had begun conferring with selected individuals in Iraq to assist him in setting up a provisional government.[27]

America's new man, L. Paul Bremer III, did two things almost immediately on arriving in Baghdad to replace Garner. One, he cashiered all of the serving Iraqi army officers; then he took the equally controversial step of nixing Garner's scheme of setting up a provisional government; Bremer said that he rather preferred to see an interim *authority* formed.[28]

This business of Bremer's wanting an authority, not a government, is crucial, and thus needs to be understood. An authority is a kind of caretaker arrangement. In the United States an authority is empowered to raise money by floating bonds and the like. The administration in the District of Columbia is an authority. Although the District may seem to fulfill the requirements of a government, in fact it is not, because it is not autonomous—Congress controls the District.

Similarly this would have been the case with Bremer's authority—and some Iraqis bridled when he put the idea forth. The scheme seemed likely to diminish, not enhance, their role under the occupation.[29] Might not it be the case that Iraqis would fill ministerial posts in the new "authority" but Americans, operating behind the scenes, would be the actual rulers?

The first public outcry against the switch came from Hakim. He said that he would withdraw his organization SCIRI from cooperating with the Americans.[30] And Bremer, assuming a hard-nosed stance, said in effect, *all right, so be it.* One would have thought that Hakim, a figure already under suspicion (in the Americans' eyes), would not have compromised himself so. If (as I am assuming) he came to Iraq to steer the process of forming a government, why opt out? The Americans must have thought, *great, we're rid of him.* If so, they misjudged their man.

We now get the first hint of trouble with Sistani. On July 1, 2003, Sistani, the quietist, the 73-year-old ayotollah who was supposed to be so retiring and so chary of involving himself in politics, abruptly came out in opposition to measures Bremer was promoting.[31] He claimed that the Iraqis must have control over their affairs and seemed to throw doubt on the Americans' motives in wanting to set up an indirect, not direct, form of governance. His objections, however, were vague, and they did not come directly from him but rather were reported by confidants. Nonetheless, by the mere fact of his having expressed misgivings, Sistani could be said to be allying with Hakim.[32]

This was bizarre; there was no apparent basis for such a relationship. Hakim and Sistani were worlds apart in their theological positions, with Hakim representing the Khomeini line, which as I said, was opposed to what Sistani (the quietist) supposedly stood for. Moreover, Sistani was a member of the Najaf School, a nucleus of ayatollahs based in the Iraqi city of Najaf, who presumed to dictate policy for all Shiadom. The rival school—to which Hakim belonged—was in Qum, Iran. Competition between Najaf and Qum goes back quite a ways. It did not make sense that Sistani would take the side of someone like Hakim, who could have been considered his arch rival.

I think Sistani was coerced by Hakim.[33] Along with everything else, Sistani had the reputation of being—what Americans would call—a weak sister: he could not stand criticism, and quite a bit of it had begun circulating about him (which may have been a campaign orchestrated by Iran). The old man could not have been made easy in his mind seeing a colleague, Khoi, hacked to death, practically on his (Sistani's) doorstep.[34]

In any event, had it just been Sistani and Hakim giving trouble, the Americans might have found a way out of this impasse. But a couple of other prominent expatriates now waded into the dispute, taking the side of Hakim (and Sistani). Before I go into detail on this I want to say something about the expatriates in general.

I said above that when Hakim arrived in Iraq his way was prepared because he had, since 1999, been in America's good books, so to speak, one of the original seven exiled Iraqis whom Indyk had championed.

It may seem odd that Indyk would support someone such as Hakim. However, it is understandable in light of the situation that originally obtained back then. After the first Iraq War, the United States had expected the Ba'thists to be overthrown, and they and the British had tried to help the situation along by imposing sanctions on Iraq, the idea being that restrictions, inasmuch as they would make life difficult for Iraqis, would induce them to turn against their government.

When that did not happen; when the Ba'thists succeeded, not only in holding on to power but also in consolidating their hold, voices began being raised in the United Nations and elsewhere to lift the sanctions, which clearly were hurting the Iraqi people.

Indyk, then, to still these pleas, formed the Iraqi opposition front, comprising seven individuals, whom he invited to Washington where he encouraged them to speak out on the suppositious injustices of the Ba'th. Indyk fostered the view that these seven, as heads of their respective organizations, comprised the authentic voice of Iraqis, who could not speak for themselves for fear of the Mukhabarat.

As a consequence of all this, the seven acquired a cachet: in Washington they were looked on as freedom fighters. Like Chalabi they were welcome visitors to the American Enterprise Institute, the Washington Institute for

Near East Policy, and other right-wing and Zionist think tanks. When the second Iraq war ended victoriously (for the Americans), all seven rushed back to Iraq, expecting to take up positions in the new government.[35] And indeed Garner seems to have let them know that he would support their claims to play leading roles in any government he might form.

The seven were Hakim and another Iranian client; Ibrahim al Jaafari, of the Dawa Party (Dawa is, like SCIRI, an Iranian surrogate); the two Kurdish leaders, Jelal Talabani of the PUK and Massoud Barzani of the KDP; Iyad Allawi of the Iraqi National Congress (INC); Chalabi; and finally there was a member of the Iraqi Communist Party.

What would have motivated Indyk to include in the front someone who was a Communist? Interesting question, also apposite. To me, the presence of the Communists gives the game away. I do not believe that the front ever stood for much; that is, I do not believe that anyone in the Clinton administration took it seriously. It was put together purely for public relations purposes, to deflect criticism of the sanctions.[36]

That a Communist was included can be explained thusly. The intelligence community for years drafted so-called opposition studies which kept tabs on various figures and groups opposed to the Ba'th. Five of the seven organizations (SCIRI, Dawa, the PUK and KDP, and the Communist Party) singled out by Indyk were regularly included in these write ups. Among intelligence officers, the opposition studies were always something of a problem. The officers were aware that opposition to the Ba'th was thin on the ground, so to speak. None of the groups written up had a following in Iraq, and one—the Communist Party—was actually defunct. (Reason for the Iraqis' indifference to the expatriates derived from their having lived so long out-of-country: Chalabi had been away for 50 years).

So it would appear that Indyk merely had plucked the names out of a hat; and in the process of so doing had conferred on the oppositionists a status to which they were not entitled. Back in Washington a regular cheering squad developed to talk these people up, principally among the right-wing think tanks. (In Iraq, Hussein and the Ba'thists ridiculed them, saying that no one there knew who they were.)

At any event, the expatriates were all back in Baghdad when the dispute with the Occupation Authority blew up and it was the two Kurdish leaders who now came out in opposition to Bremer, along with Sistani and Hakim. Talabani and Barzani objected to the idea of substituting an authority for a government.

What caused the Kurdish personalties to go into opposition? I think it was self-interest. Talabani and Barzani, as with the other expatriates, had gotten in on the ground floor of a good thing. They were present at the creation of the new Iraq, and thus were positioned to exploit the situation. Now, along comes Bremer and says, the idea of forming a government, while well intentioned, ought to be put on the back burner for awhile. *For how long?*

One year? Two years? A lot can happen in that space of time. The expatriates' special relationships with the Americans could erode over so long a period.

In coming out on the side of Hakim in the dispute with Bremer, the Kurds appear to have been colluding with the Iranian contingent: the right hand would wash the left, so to speak; by allying, the expatriates would have more clout opposing the proconsul.

That is speculation on my part—but I know of no other reason why the Kurds, whom the Americans had assumed were solidly in their corner, would, as I say, defect, and make trouble for Bremer.

We now want to get into the specifics of Sistani's objections. Mainly he opposed Bremer's notion of having a council handpicked by the proconsul write the constitution. Sistani wanted an election to seat a government, which then would do the constitution writing. He also wanted the whole process of forming a government speeded up.

Bremer wanted to slow-march the move towards democracy. He argued that, Iraq, having had no experience of this type of system, ran a risk of pieing the type, so to speak. What would happen if the democratization process failed? That would be a disaster. Therefore, in Bremer's scenario, the Iraqis should move *gradually* toward setting up a new government.

To accomplish this slowdown, Bremer wanted to divide the transfer of power into stages. First, the Iraqis would form a council of 25 individuals, whom Bremer would appoint. These 25 would oversee the creation of a National Assembly of over 200 Iraqis charged with actually writing the constitution, which would then be approved by a national referendum, and then—and only then—national elections would be held.[37] The whole process could take up to two years.

As to why Sistani objected to this cautious approach, he gave no clue. Although, as we will see, Bremer's scheme was not only threatening to ambitions he might have, it also complicated maneuvers Hakim and the Iranians were undertaking.

Perhaps because he was caught off guard by the suddenness with which the opposition developed (after all, the Occupation Authority was only two months old), Bremer agreed to scale back his proposals. He would not budge on the council idea (that was a sine qua non, he said), but he did agree that the council should have more power.[38] He would let the new administration (as he called it) recommend (his word) on matters such as establishing a currency; setting oil policy; laying out an economic strategy; and instituting reform of the education system.

Administration; recommend? Bremer was using terms that related to an *authority,* not a *government,* and it was the authority idea that the expatriates were most vocally objecting to. They did not want an authority; they wanted a *government,* something which they thought they already had—or at least that was in the process of forming. As far as they were concerned, any tinkering with the already existing setup worked against them. Bremer, by scrapping the idea of a government, was sidelining them, or so it appeared.

One of the minor mysteries of the American occupation is why Bremer would have crossed swords with the expatriates; why did he not just let things ride?[39] The expatriates were most of them well connected to the Washington power establishment, or so they claimed. Chalabi was relentlessly going on about his ties to the neo-cons and through the neo-cons to the Israelis. Talabani and Barzani similarly were tied in with the American-Israeli Political Action Committee (AIPAC), and Allawi was widely regarded as the CIA's man.[40]

I think—and this is more speculation on my part—that Garner was perceived (back in Washington) as moving in a wrong direction: inasmuch as native Iraqis appeared to be shut out of the government-formation process. Garner was allowing the expatriates, in a manner of speaking, to run the show.

The Americans going into Iraq had had a daunting problem to confront, namely, that Iraq was a totalitarian state, one where the Ba'th Party ran everything. There were no competing parties (indeed under such a system there could not have been). So how then do you draw the populace into the process of forming a government?

Before the victory the Americans seemed not to have been overly concerned about this. Thanks to Wolfowitz, Feith, and the rest of the neo-cons, Bush had been led to believe that the Iraqis (the Kurds, certainly, but also the Shias) would jump for joy when the invading force entered the country. Instead of that, as I have already shown, the Shias and Sunnis fought to oppose it. So now the Americans had a big worry: whom do we find to work with us?

What basically had gone wrong, I think, was that the Americans really did believe that they had suborned key Iraqi army commanders, and it was these people they were intending to elevate to high posts in the new government, once formed. I think they also expected the police to cooperate in the invasion. When the putative defections failed to materialize—when the army men and police remained at their posts, and even took part in the last stand of the Ba'th in Baghdad—the failure was keenly felt on the American side.

The Americans may have overreacted: in a pet, they decided to junk plans to work with the army and police, and in effect proscribed them. Then, when the anarchy developed, they saw how badly off they were: with no natives signed up as collaborators, how to win the "hearts and minds" of the people? Which Iraqis was it safe to co-opt? I think that is what was behind Bremer's scheme of trying to draw out the process of government formation. It would give the Americans time to size up the Iraqis, locate the good, i.e., dependable ones, and then, when they had identified a number of such individuals, put them in charge of the country.

The mistake the Americans made was in assuming that the good Iraqis would automatically stand forth; that is that they would advance their candidacy for co-optation. To be sure, a number did, and had there been no expatriates to contend with something might have been worked out. Unfortunately, after living for years under the Ba'th, the native Iraqis had no idea how to politic; in a phrase they had not a clue how things were done under a democracy.

The expatriates, on the other hand, were all wheeler-dealers. Particularly, the Kurds had long experience working with AIPAC, and they had an "in" with Garner.

Immediately the expatriates began sniping away at Bremer, accusing him of reversing the march towards democracy; they even accused him of trying to set up a puppet government, complaints that were transmitted to the western press corps in Baghdad.

Most destructive for the reforms Bremer was trying to effect the expatriates spread it about (and here is where Chalabi was particularly active) that all of the "good Iraqis" Bremer was seeking to cultivate were ex-Ba'thists, and therefore ineligible for posts in the new government; they should not even be brought in for consultations, Chalabi said.

Had the Americans gone to Iraq with a more clear-cut idea of what they wanted to accomplish, I think they would have managed. But obviously they had no such set purpose.

Before the invasion, Wolfowitz, in essaying to put his leadership team together, had had only two months to prepare. Then, the team went out and it soon became obvious the technocrats were ill prepared: they could not hack the politics of getting established any more than could the native Iraqis. The team in no time melted away—the technocrats seem to have drifted back to the states.

Meanwhile a turf war raged in Washington between the Defense and State Departments as to who was going to run the occupation, both sides put forth schemes, which, once advanced, became set in concrete. For Defense and State, the fight over who was to run Iraq was a zero-sum game. If flaws were discovered in one's plan, no one would admit to that; this would give a leg up to the "enemy."[41]

Finally, there was Chalabi. The neo-cons' man pursued such a tortuous course in Iraq it is almost impossible to figure out what he was up to. He seems to have been a double agent of sorts, or maybe even a triple one. Before too much time had elapsed he apparently deserted the American side to go over to the Iranians, something which should have been unthinkable, but nonetheless seems to have happened.[42] In any case, if the Bush administration relied on Chalabi for advice, it was getting a bum steer.

In other words, the expatriates were politicians, and they shrewdly manipulated public opinion in the United States to get their way. The native Iraqis were babes in the woods compared to them.

Another point I want to make is every one of the expatriates who survived to become later a figure of importance in the new government (and they all did finally wangle leadership roles for themselves) had his own private army: Hakim and Jaafari had the Badr Brigades; Talabani, the PUK; Barzani, the KDP; Allawi had the Iraqi National Accord (INA), and Chalabi the INC. All these sound like political parties. They were not. They were armed militias, the institution which subsequently was to become the bane of the Americans' existence.

In any event, as soon as the Kurdish leaders lined up with the pro-Iranian faction (Hakim and Jaafari), Bremer was compromised, seriously so. He now had the suppositious leaders of the two most important communities in Iraq allied against him (the neo-cons, from the first, were dead set against cultivating the Sunnis in any way). Bremer may have believed he had Sistani; that Sistani was nonaligned, but that, as far as I can figure, was a delusion—Sistani was in Hakim's pocket, all of his subsequent actions go to prove that.

The supreme irony was that *what the expatriates wanted for Iraq was against everything the Americans supposedly were trying to accomplish there: the expatriates wanted to weaken Iraq, not strengthen it.* Hakim and Jaafari wanted to subsume the country (at least the southern portion of it) within Iran's sphere of influence.[43] (Chalabi, too, apparently had come around to this view). And the two Kurdish expatriate leaders, Talabani and Barzani, wanted to outright destroy the state, by carving a separate Kurdish entity out of it.

One can argue that this was wrong, morally wrong; that the Americans had an obligation, under international law, to maintain the integrity of Iraq. That is true, they did. But there was something more crucial involved: weakening the state was going to compound the problems besetting the occupation. With an inadequate force the Americans could barely cope as it was. They therefore needed support from inside the country.

Among Iraqis (and not a few Middle Easterners), the conviction grew that America had had it in mind all along to destroy Iraq. The conspiracy theorists pointed to the anomaly of Washington favoring the expatriates, all of whom—with maybe two exceptions—did actually advocate such a result.

I do not go along with this line of reasoning. I believe that things went wrong because the Americans, feeling they had to act in haste (in invading Iraq), had abandoned good sense.[44] They did not do their homework; they did not call on the expertise of area specialists back in the United States, and most of all, the Bush administration refused to do damage control—except for sending Bremer out, there was no attempt to rectify mistakes, and, as we just saw, even Bremer went to Iraq with a lot of wrong suppositions.

Meanwhile the Iranians appear to have worked out their strategy down to the finest detail. This would explain the rapidity with which SCIRI, Dawa, and the Badr Brigades appeared on the scene. It would explain the quick dispatch of Khoi, hacked to death in Najaf (that is if you credit that Hakim ordered the murder, which I do). It would explain the unanticipated *volte face* of Sistani.

And, finally, it could even be an explanation for the shift of the Kurdish leaders. This last is somewhat problematic, since it implies the Kurds were plotting with the Iranians from the first. However, there is some evidence for this. When Hakim entered Iraq just after the victory, he came accompanied by his militiamen, many of whom entered through the North, the Kurdish region; they took this route because that section of the border is difficult to patrol, it being all high mountains. However, even so, had the Kurdish warlords wanted to interdict the entry of Hakim's people, they could have done so.[45] They did not. Why? I think it reasonable to suppose that Talabani, at least, was already as far back as this hedging his bets, positioning himself so that he could jump to the side of Iran if things went badly for the Americans.[46]

Something else that seems to bear on this: Sistani, I said, was a recluse, he would see no one—not even Bremer. *But he saw Barzani.* The day before Sistani came out with his initial objection to Bremer's scheme, he received Barzani at his palace in Najaf. Barzani came away claiming that Sistani was unhappy with Bremer's proposals, the first indication of such opposition.

Far fetched? Not when you consider that both the Kurdish warlords were clients of the Iranians throughout the Iran-Iraq war. Both had been instrumental in trying to open a second front in the North, which, as I said in the last chapter, had it succeeded would have sunk the Iraqis.

This to me is the most astonishing aspect of the whole business: that the Americans, in allowing the expatriates to achieve such prominence, never took into account that the two Kurdish leaders—as was the case with the two Shias—*had fought on Iran's side in that war.* How must it have appeared to the native Iraqis that individuals who had fought against them, and whom they had driven out of Iraq (when the Iran-Iraq War ended), were now back in the country claiming the right to run it?

We saw in the last chapter how the Basrawis reacted to the reappearance of the Badr Brigades, swanning around, giving orders. I theorized that Sadr's call for revolt was well received in the South because of the developing situation there (with the Brigades). It was as if the Americans had never heard of the Iran-Iraq War; did not know the particulars of what went on in it. At any rate, it certainly was a big slap in the face (to the Iraqis) to install quislings (of Iran) in the rule over them.

Why could not Bush simply have called a halt; said, whoa; enough is enough; we are not going there? And then calmly and deliberately set about creating a situation the United States could control?

Several factors seem to have operated here. On the one hand, the Americans were conscious that, in the world's eyes, they had performed a powergrab. Bush had deliberately excluded the United Nations from having anything to do with the takeover. He had even *dissed* some of America's closest allies, who had volunteered to assist. This was done, the conspiracy theorists judged, so that America could latch onto the country's rich oil reserves.

Anxious to dispel any such notion, Washington did all in its power to convey the perception that it was working with the Iraqis, taking their wishes into account. This seems to have been the thrust of Garner's approach when he announced that he would put together a provisional *government* and convene a congress of prominent Iraqis to discuss how this could be done.

Then Bremer was sent out and everything was put on hold. Bremer defended his determination to slow down the process of establishing a government by claiming (as I said) that he feared the Iraqis were rushing things; he claimed that he had their best interests at heart, since he wanted to be sure a true democracy would emerge, one that worked. The expatriates countered with a barrage of complaints to the western press corps, making it out that the proconsul was trying to take control of affairs away from Iraqis.

It was a perfect storm of trouble for the Americans, and one they were not up to withstanding. In a test between the expatriates and Bremer—who was pretty much on his own—the expatriates won hands down. *Tant pis,* as the French would say.

Another factor which influenced the Americans to go along was Bush's insistence the democratization had to be seen to be working. Once it developed that there were no WMD, Bush and Blair were embarrassed. If there was no threat, why did they invade? Their defense was they did it for the Iraqis. They were responding to appeals to remove the tyrant Hussein, and to give the Iraqis the benefits of democratic rule.

Playing the democratization card had become a matter of some urgency as public opinion in the United States had begun turning against the administration (not to mention the public opinion swing in Britain, which was worse). Americans saw that pacification was not working; the resistance was growing. Hence Bush needed some way of steadying the home front, of assuring Americans that things were going to be all right. Over the course of months, he lay down markers: as soon as Hussein was captured (he said) that would make the resistance collapse; as soon as a provisional government was formed, things would improve, and so on.

In other words, Bush was making it out that democratization was the panacea. The Iraqis, in gratitude for having been permitted to form their own government, would soon start to cooperate with the occupiers. However, in fostering that impression the administration overlooked what was happening on the ground. After every one of Bush's milestone events came off, the violence actually spiked.

What *was* going on? Mainly this: the procedures the Americans were being induced to adopt sabotaged their ability to control events inside the country.

The chronology of the debacle goes like so. Sistani expressed his objections to Bremer's proposals initially, as I said, in a closed meeting with Barzani. He then adopted a more formal stance one week later when he issued a *fetwa,* this is a religious ruling, and as such is supposed to be binding on Muslims.[47] The fetwa essentially enjoined Mulsims from cooperating with the Occupation Authority.

As soon as the fetwa appeared, large demonstrations of Shias materialized in the streets of Baghdad, Najaf, and Basrah (these could have been, and probably were, orchestrated by the Iranians). In these, Bremer was condemned, and there were actual appeals for the Americans to leave the country.

Whether it was the demonstrations that coerced him, I do not know. But Bremer effectively caved in not too soon afterward. He agreed that the council he was determined to form could be called a *governing* council.[48] As such, it would be empowered to appoint a cabinet. Iraqis chosen by the Council members would take over the various ministries in Baghdad, while the Americans would keep control of finances and of course the U.S. military would continue to look out for security.

In making this change, Bremer also agreed that the expatriates would form the core of the new body, meaning they would choose the cabinet members. Along with that he decreed that membership on the Council would be apportioned along ethnic lines, with the Shias getting 13 seats out of 25, the Kurds five, and the Sunnis five—with two other seats slated for a woman and a member of the Turkoman community.[49]

Now, two things were accomplished by this. First, the expatriates succeeded in institutionalizing their role. Up to this point they technically had no official standing; although they might claim to be bona fide leaders, they had no defined position. Now they had it; they were on their way to exercising the role they coveted; that is, of being power brokers.

The second "accomplishment" is more important. With his concession to structure the Council along ethnic lines, Bremer was preparing the ground for an unmanageable system. It is not generally understood in the United States how the Ba'th party was able to control Iraq. The received wisdom (and it is wrong, as received wisdom often tends to be) is that it ruled through fear; it tortured, it killed—it made Iraqis cringe in dread of their lives, and that way the Ba'thists kept themselves in power.

Actually the true explanation (as I tried to bring out in Chapters 2 and 3) was more devious. The Ba'th came to power at a time when Iraqis were exhausted from all the terror of the early days of the republic.

At the time they came to power, the Ba'thists' chances of maintaining control were up in the air, so to speak; they had no more popular support than previous governments. However, they made one shrewd move which pretty much, I would say, saved their bacon: they carried through on the oil nationalization, with the result that, when, four years after the party took power the OPEC Revolution hit, the Ba'th was sitting pretty: it owned the oil fields, and it had imported Soviet technicians to bring them up to a satisfactory level of production. Thus the Ba'thists began pulling in enormous amounts of revenue. They made sure that a lot of this was spent on improving the lives of the average Iraqi.

Then, the party created this huge bureaucracy and brought in the East German Stassi, to honeycomb it with paid informants, or, in some instances, Iraqis who merely worked for perks.

As a result, the Ba'th created a superefficient police state.

But, and this is the important part, in adopting this carrot-and-stick policy (which is essentially what it was) of spending money on Iraqis and hiring them to fill jobs in the bureaucracy while putting them under intense surveillance and cracking down hard when they strayed out of line, the Ba'th resolved what always was the number one problem governing the Iraqis.

From roughly the time of the British on, Iraq faced an almost insoluble problem of demographics. The birth rate kept steadily climbing. Iraq has the most youthful population in the Middle East. This youth component forms a restless mass. Moreover, pretty much all of the erstwhile institutions which formerly had been useful to control Iraq had over the years lost influence. For example, the British had carried forward a process of weakening the tribal system, based on work already done by the Turks. And the Ba'th seriously weakened the power of the clergy. No longer bound to their villages, young Iraqis gravitated to the capital looking for work. Baghdad developed into one huge metropolis, a magnet for the poor (remember, I spoke of the Shurugi problem).

The Hashmites could never control the urban mobs, and neither could the early republican regimes. The Ba'th did, but only because they had jobs to deal out; that and their Stasi-developed system to keep people in line.

Now, how does all this relate to the principle of ethnicity in determining the future structure of the occupation? The last thing the Americans wanted was to create competition to their exercise of control, and of course were they to allow the formation of two power blocs (the Kurds and Shias; the neo-cons having fixed it so the Sunnis did not count) that was precisely what they were bound to do.

By creating a system of communal proportionality, the Americans were sabotaging their own efforts to take charge. The new system started the process of breaking Iraq down into divisions: a Shia bloc, ruled over by the ayatollahs (in collusion with the Iranians), and a smaller Kurdish bloc—and as for the Sunnis, they were purposely left out in the cold.

At this stage in the narrative all this was still in the offing. But, as we will soon see, from this point on, from Bremer's decision to apportion seats on the Council along ethnic lines, things in Iraq started moving steadily downhill for the Americans.

Having given way on this one key point, Bremer soon was compelled to make other fateful concessions. The reader will recall that originally he wanted the process of transferring rule in Iraq to be carried out in three stages: first off, he wanted the council to select an assembly to write a constitution, then after the constitution was written and approved, step three would have been the holding of elections. Now, the Council members (which is to say, the expatriates, since they were in charge) wanted the elections to come first, and then the new government would write the constitution. Through all of this, note what the expatriates were fussing over: *it was the provision of writing a constitution!*

In retrospect it is easy to see why they were concerned: practically all the expatriates were pushing agendas they dared not divulge. The Kurdish politicians wanted to hive off the North of Iraq to form a separate state. They masked this determination by claiming what they really wanted was a form of federalism; that is a system where Iraq would be split into cantons (along the lines of the system in Switzerland), with a Kurdish portion and an Arab one. But along with this they also wanted Kirkuk, a city on the edge of the Kurdish territory, where a goodly proportion of Iraq's oil is located, to be subsumed under the Kurdish area.[50]

That is a pretty explosive proposition. The Turks will not allow the creation of an independent Kurdish state, especially one which controlled the oil.[51] Turkey contains the largest Kurdish minority in the Middle East, several million, all located in the Southeast. For years that part of the country has been deprived, hence considerable resentment obtains between Turkish Kurds and their government. Were the Iraqi Kurds to get an independent (and viable, because of the oil) state, bank on it, the Turkish Kurds would want one too, and were a strong separatist movement to emerge in Turkey, that could destroy the state. So, under no circumstances were the Kurds willing to spell out the details of their plan, which they would have had to do were they to write a constitution.

Similarly the two Shia parties, SCIRI and Dawa, were not anxious to publicize the sort of government they were seeking: they wanted Iraq to become an adjunct of the Islamic Republic; and they wanted to bring this about by harmonizing the two systems (Iran's and Iraq's): Iraq would become a theocracy.

To avoid having to put their cards on the table, the expatriates contrived to stall, pushing the actual constitution writing farther and farther into the future, while they were busy consolidating their control.

At the same time, the expatriates were clever enough not to overplay their hand. For awhile they kept a low profile. They seemed to back away from their demand that a government be formed, ASAP. As far as Bremer was concerned, they were fulfilling their assigned task of writing the constitution. In the meantime they preened. On September 2, 2003, they held an initial session of their new governing council, appearing at a building set aside for them, all tricked out in their robes and finery (the religious figures in their turbans, the tribal leaders in their *gallabeyas*).[52] Naturally, as might have been expected, the session was opened with a prayer, the Muslim equivalent of one.

However, almost immediately after that the expatriates announced that the writing of a constitution was simply beyond them. They claimed that this was something in which all Iraqis should be involved—a way of appearing to take the high road; professing to be looking out for their fellows; seeing to it that they had a voice in government. In fact, the last thing the expatriates wanted was to empower the native Iraqis. Hence, their opposition to the Iraqi Shias, represented by Moktada, and their clever manipulation of the Sunni issue, claiming all Sunnis were actually Ba'thists and hence ineligible for posts in the government.

At this point Secretary of State Colin Powell stepped in, giving the Council members six months to do the job they had been tasked to perform. Also, the United Nations backed up Powell's demand, saying the constitution was essential.[53]

In mid-November, Bremer flew back to Washington, where, in an unscheduled meeting in the White House, he informed Bush that the Council was deadlocked; it would not give way on the matter of drafting the constitution. Bremer even used the word "revolt": the Council was on the point of revolting, he said.[54]

With that, Bush did an about face and agreed that the order of progression whereby Iraq would move to self governing status would be reversed. The elections would be held in the beginning of January 2005, and the constitution would follow after that. In the meantime, the Iraqis were to be accorded sovereignty by June of 2004. This meant they would set policy for controlling the country's wealth and perform other tasks initially reserved for the occupation authority. (The Council also wanted to take over security, claiming the right to order American troops out of cities if they deemed that this was necessary. The Americans balked on that one—but otherwise the sovereignty hand over was to be more or less complete.)

Why the surrender? Two things probably came into play. Bush was looking forward to elections himself in the new year, and he evidently thought it essential to show movement on the Iraq front. Moreover, at this juncture Iraq was experiencing extreme turbulence; it was one of the more violent periods since victory was declared. The insurgency was picking up steam and spreading despite the Americans' efforts to tamp it down. Two months before the transfer of authority was to take place, at the end of March 2004, Fallujah exploded and right after that Bremer decided to go after Moktada, and thus the Shias loyal to the youthful cleric, they, too, were up in arms. As a consequence, when the transfer came off in June 2004, Iraq was roiling with turmoil.

Up to this point my narrative tracks closely with that of the last chapter where I described the growth of the Iraqi insurgency. Now, however, the character of the revolt undergoes a profound change. It becomes something more closely resembling a civil war, where the various communities in Iraq found themselves pitted against each other.

When the elections for the new government came off in January 2005, the procedure whereby they were conducted departed significantly from Bremer's original plan. Bremer had wanted there to be caucuses, which he, along with the governors of the 18 provinces of Iraq, would appoint. These caucuses would take charge of holding the elections. Had that scheme been followed, power in Iraq would have devolved to the provincial level; it would have had the effect of defusing it more or less equally across the country. In other words, the over-determining factor would have been local politics.

As it worked out in practice, however, the old bugaboo of ethnicity reasserted itself. Sistani weighed in again just before the elections were to take place with a demand they be conducted on a basis of one man, one vote. It sounded good. But, in fact, in a country like Iraq, where three large, mutually suspicious communities exist, to structure the elections so practically ensured that there would be voting along ethnic lines. It also, of course, ensured that the Shias, with 60 percent of the population, would pile up a majority. This appears to have been the Iranians' game plan; why they were so eager from the first for elections to be held—they believed that the Shias, constituting as they did a majority, would sweep the field. Before the elections came off, Abdul Aziz al Hakim (who had taken over SCIRI after his brother was killed) announced the formation of a United Shia Alliance, which he headed. His plan evidently was to corral the native Iraqi Shias into voting for the Alliance, which effectively would deliver the vote to Iran.

It is difficult to evaluate the elections, because there were so many irregularities. Nonetheless, the Iranians' scheme was somewhat thwarted because Moktada at the last minute signalled his entry into the field, and given his popularity among the natives, he split the Shia vote, grabbing a significant portion for himself. Still the Alliance easily secured a place in the government, although, as I say, it is impossible to say how much of its vote was legitimate.

It was brought out after the elections that the Iranians had sent a lot of ringers across the border to vote illegally (the vote was a hurried job, and as a result the Occupation Authority had failed to put together an accurate voting list.)[55] The Sunnis boycotted; they would not legitimize the elections by participating in them, which meant they lost out all around. Something else, largely overlooked by the western media, which influenced the outcome was that just before the elections the Americans conducted sweeps, rounding up and putting in jail suspected terrorists—maybe up to 10,000 of them—and most were Sunnis; of course, being in prison they could not vote.[56] And finally under the setup agreed to by the Americans, expatriates could vote; that meant Iraqis living in Iran, and even former Iraqis living in Israel (most of whom left Iraq after the 1948 war) were eligible.[57] And how did they vote? Of course, we do not know, but I would presume in the case of the Iranian contingent it would have been for the pro-Iranian slate.

In any event, it ought to have come as no surprise that all of the expatriates wound up in positions of power. Talabani (PUK) became the new president of Iraq; Ibrahim al Jaafari (Dawa), the prime minister; Abdul Aziz al Hakim (SCIRI) controlled the United Shia Alliance, which I consider the instrument of Iran; Barzani (KDP) took over as head of the Kurdish parliament in the North. Alawi (INC) became the prime minister (the prime minister position originally rotated), and finally Chalabi (ANC) got the oil ministry!

The overall result? Instead of integrating the country and reinforcing its coherence, the elections promoted the tendency by which Iraq has been beset throughout its history; that is, for the state to fly apart.

What we witness next is a significant (and, in retrospect, sinister) shifting of ground by the native Iraqis. I mentioned earlier that after every one of Bush's milestone events was logged, the violence in Iraq, instead of diminishing, actually spiked. No one could account for this. I do not see why not—it seems apparent what was going on. The native Iraqis, as they began to perceive the direction that things were tending, grew more and more apprehensive. In one regard, Iraq is not much different from the United States: the assignment of portfolios in the government shows the future course of policy. If a Christian fundamentalist right-winger is assigned the post of head of the Justice Department, that is certain to rile American liberals. In the Middle East, probably the two most powerful portfolios (in any government, not just Iraq) are the Defense and Interior Ministries. In Iraq, Defense is not so important since the Americans supply the military force. *But Interior?* Interior is the police in Middle Eastern lands!

Immediately after the elections it was announced that a member of SCIRI, was to get the Interior Ministry. This was Bayan Jabr. The ex-officers greeted this announcement by going for their guns, an altogether justifiable reaction, I feel. The officers had fought SCIRI and the Badr Brigades throughout the Iran-Iraq War. In 1991, Iran sent the Badr Brigades into Iraq to start a revolt among the Iraqi Shias in Basrah. It was the Iraqi army that put down that would-be revolt, killing many of the brigadistas—indeed the mass graves outside of Basrah, uncovered after the American invasion, largely are filled with the corpses of brigadistas whom the army had dispatched. Now, a member of SCIRI was to take over the Interior, which would set the Iranians up to exact revenge.

Similarly, Moktada had to fear the appointment of Jabr. Moktada, if you will recall, was accused of having killed Muhamad Bakr al Hakim, SCIRI's

former head. Thus he too faced retribution. To be sure, Moktada was somewhat protected, insofar as he had decided to work within the system by
fielding a party in the elections. But still, he obviously was discomforted by
having an Iranian stooge (as he would have viewed the matter) directing
the country's security apparatus. The natives, which would have included
Moktada's people, did not want a lot of revanchists deciding life and death
issues for them.

The natives' fears were immediately confirmed as soon after the elections
were held, and the new government formed, it was announced that a delegation would be sent to Tehran to meet with the mullahs, with the announced
intention of "developing good relations between neighbor states." At this
meeting it was revealed that Iran *would help train the new Iraqi army and
police* (they also announced they were going to build a pipeline to carry oil
from Iraq's southern fields to Iran.)[58]

The reader can perhaps appreciate the effect of this on the natives.
Iran, with the backing of the United States, was undoing its defeat in the
Iran-Iraq War. Under the Ba'th, the Iraqis had fought the Iranians and
triumphed—a come-from-behind victory of which Iraqis were justly proud.
And now, thanks to the Americans, the Iranians were in control of their
country, imposing a victor's peace, *on them.*

Moreover, the new Iraqi government announced that it was going to
put on trial Saddam Hussein and a number of other top Ba'thists, *including
several Iraqi army officers.* This created an international furor, as the world
community, whereas it would have approved a trial such as that conducted
in Yugoslavia, where the United Nations took charge, was dead set against
the Iraqi government doing so—primarily because the government insisted
on upholding the death penalty.

Bush claimed that it was only right that the Iraqis should try Hussein, and
his fellow Ba'thists. But how fair was the trial? In fact it was a circus. Three
defense attorneys were killed; witnesses for the defense were intimidated—
in some cases jailed after they had given evidence for the defense, and made
to recant. And two judges were removed, because the government claimed
they were favoring the defendants.

In the end, all of the defendants took the same line: what they did,
they did for Iraq.[59] Hussein, of course, was executed as was his half brother
Barzan, in particularly grumsome style. At Hussein's trial the crowd let into
watch the execution taunted him by shouting: Muhammad Bakr al Sadr (the
uncle of Moktada executed by Hussein). In Barzan's case, he was actually
decapitated by the roughness with which he was dispatched.

As I say, in Bush's view there was nothing wrong in this. But in Iraqis'
eyes, these men were being executed for having done their duty to their
country.

And now something truly dreadful occurred. Someone—it is never
been established who—blew up one of the most revered sites of Shiadom,

the Golden Mosque in Samarra. Bush claimed that this was Zarkawi. It may have been. But then it could have been anyone; it could have been the officers.[60] Who actually did the job is not important. What counts is that, given the climate of fear engendered by the composition of the new government, the attack, which under any circumstances would have excited unrest, now produced something like panic.

Quite soon after Bremer came to Iraq he made two decisions which, in retrospect, he ought never to have made. Because he could not get Rumsfeld to send more troops, he agreed to allow the Kurdish pesh mergas, that is the militias of the PUK and KDP, to keep their arms (they would help police the security situation), and he followed this up by agreeing to accord the same privilege to the Badr Brigades.[61]

These were incredibly foolish moves! Iraqis, under the Ba'th, had embraced modernism, but certain traditional modes of behavior hung on. Most notably, the vendetta. When one community perceives itself at risk from another, its reaction is to arm—in other words, to form a militia. I showed in Chapter 2 how the tradition of militias was practically engrained in the Iraqis' psyches, going back at least to the days of Qasem. Now it burst forth anew; full spate, as it were.

The first nonsanctioned group to react to the mosque episode by going into the streets with weapons was Moktada's Mahdi Army. His decision to turn out may have been opportunistic: he may have wanted to serve notice on Bayan that he was prepared to defend himself, should the ministry move against him.

However, in coming out as he did, Moktada panicked the Sunnis. That community now began to draw in on itself; the Sunnis shut themselves off from the rest of society.[62] They did this most concretely, by literally throwing up barricades, sealing off their neighborhoods, rendering them into separate enclaves. As had occurred with Fallujah, overnight formerly open areas in Baghdad became no-go zones. Not only the government, but the U.S. military was denied access.[63]

In effect, now, the focus of revolt shifted away from the provinces, from Anbar, to the capital, and there could not have been a more unwelcome development for the Americans. Recall I said that the great accomplishment of the Ba'th had been to tame the Baghdad mob. After almost 40 years of rule by the Ba'thists, Baghdad was a well-integrated community where Shias and Sunnis lived side by side in peace.

Now, the city was being ethnically jerrymandered. One could not move from one neighborhood to another without taking wide detours to avoid passing through potentially hostile parts of town.[64] In this way the situation in Baghdad became positively medieval.

As soon as this new development occurred, the Interior Ministry stepped in to try to reverse it. The police began attempting to remove the barricades, and the barricaded communities reacted with defiance. Pitched battles erupted where the beleaguered neighborhoods gave as good as they got, and this apparently caused Bayan to lose his head.

Baghdad became the scene of actual massacres. Armed gangs would enter the sealed off neighborhoods—by night—where they would apprehend and kill people, indiscriminately. At first no one knew who was doing this, but it soon became obvious that the gangs *were operating under the authority of Bayan*—in other words these were Interior Ministry-sanctioned death squads.

The Bush administration said that these massacres were being perpetrated by jihadis. To be sure Zarkawi's people may have been involved, but the practice most certainly was initiated by the Ministry. What the government was conveying by this retributive policy was its *illegitmacy*. Bush could claim anything he wanted, about how America, by toppling the Ba'th, had improved the country's condition—*it just simply was not true*: he had set Iraq back, to the period of anarchy that succeeded the overthrow of the Hashemites.

If the new government had been truly of the people—and not a collection of carpet baggers—it might have negotiated a modus vivendi whereby it could have functioned. But this government only inspired fear and mistrust in Iraqis; consequently, it had no such capability. And so it resorted to coercion, and, in a society like Iraq's, coercion incites revolt—unless, of course, like the Ba'thists, you move astutely, coupling coercive measures with benefits. The occupation authority had no means of aggrandizing the Iraqis—it had no cash that it could dispense. Services were running down; Iraqis were out of work.

Through it all, the Americans in their, I would say, opaqueness, refused to confront the reality of what was occurring. In the United States, the press turned on the Iraqis, accusing them of spurning the gift that the Americans were lavishing on them, the gift of democracy.

Democracy? Where was the democracy, when the government the Americans had installed was run from Tehran? How could foreign agents and opportunists (because that is what the expatriates were) claim support of the Iraqis? What was required was for some strong individual, whom the Iraqis held in awe, to go among them—as Hussein was wont to do—pressing the flesh, reassuring them by his presence.

At the time when this was happening Jelal Talabani was president. And who was he; what was his pedigree?

I have a personal connection with Talabani. In 1963 I interviewed him in Tehran, as part of my series for *The Milwaukee Journal*.[65] Thus I was able to form an estimate of the man. Over the years, as an intelligence officer I continued to follow his career. In a manner of speaking, Talabani has been all over the map. At various times he worked for the Shah, for Khomeini, for Assad of Syria; he even, as I indicated above, worked for Hussein, who appointed him governor of Sulaymaniyah. He also was/is a big friend of

Israel. For a politician that is a pretty checkered career, and not anything that would dispose an Iraqi to obey, much less revere him.

Talabani has no standing in Iraqis' eyes. (They call him the chameleon, because he has changed coats so many times). As might have been expected under the circumstances, when the country erupted, Talabani virtually hid out in the North, in Arbil, never straying outside the Kurdish area.[66]

So, once again, as in April 2004, the Americans were left to secure the situation *on their own.*

Back in the United States the press put out the story that Iraq was succumbing to sectarian strife. Of course in a way it was. But why was it happening? Not because Sunnis viscerally hated Shias; or the Kurds, Arabs, because the same phenomenon developed in the North, as the Kurds sought to ethnically cleanse Kirkuk (not only of Arabs but of Turkomans).[67] The violence was a product of fear, the age old fear of people who have come to believe that their government is inimical to them, and therefore they are motivated to take the law into their own hands.

Some time after this, the secretary general of the United Nations, Kofi Annan, compared the situation in Iraq when Hussein was in charge to the way it is now under the Americans. Annan said that Iraqis were safer under the Ba'th.[68] I think it was.

According to a UN report, more Iraqi civilians died in October 2006 than in any other month since the American invasion—3,709. Most of these died at the hands of militias.[69]

Condoleezza Rice, in answer to Annan, said that Iraq was going through "the birth pangs of becoming democratized."[70] That statement was greeted with derision throughout the Middle East. And right after that U.S. Major General William Cauldwell, the chief military spokesman in Baghdad, made a similar statement, saying that Iraq should be viewed as "an art work in progress." This on a day when 49 people died or were found dead around the country.[71]

It would appear that up until this point the Americans had made every mistake in the book. Not so. There was one more fillip to this dismal saga. I said above that the U.S. military retained responsibility for the security situation. All very well, but the American force was inadequate to cope. As the violence escalated, it became more and more stressed.

As far back as July 2003, Bremer had announced that he favored the formation of a new army, which Iraqis were invited to join, and many did join (because they needed the money, many of them being destitute).[72] In the early days, this new army performed most discreditably. Recruits would not undertake distasteful assignments. They would not, for example, act against fellow sectarians: Shias would not act against Shias; Sunnis, against Sunnis. Moreover, many of the recruits turned out to be resistance plants. They had been infiltrated into the new army by the insurgency to help it lay ambushes, plant bombs, and inform on the Americans.

Once it developed that the new army composed of natives was not effective, Bremer found himself at a loss. The administration in Washington had made this out to be the grand solution to Iraq's ills ("America will stand down, when the Iraqis stand up"). Supposedly this was going to compensate for the inadequacy of America's military commitment.

Now, since the army scheme had not worked, Bremer changed tack—he agreed to a plan proposed by the expatriates whereby they would "lend" their private armies to the Occupation Authority; in other words the pro-Iranian militias (Shia and Kurdish) would be enfolded into the new army. It is almost beyond belief that Bremer would not have seen the danger this posed. But considering the way that things were going, he may have felt he had no alternative.[73]

Previously, by permitting certain militias to go about openly armed, Bremer had awakened primal fears in the Iraqis. At the same time, as long as there was a national army, separate and distinct from the militias, this fear was mitigated, somewhat. *But now the militias were the army.*

It should not have surprised anyone that after this all hell broke loose. It did most certainly appear that Iraq was descending into civil war.

And was it? I do not know. Like practically everything else that has gone on in the country, no neat characterization seems to apply. For example, commentators have compared the situation in Iraq to Lebanon in the 1970s–1980s. But in Lebanon slight chance existed that the state would deconstruct. To be sure the Israelis worked hard to make it happen, and so, one could say, did the Syrians. But the Lebanese remained reasonably solidaric throughout their ordeal.

In the case of Iraq, as I have tried to show, forces from *within* the state are agitating to break it apart. There are the Kurdish warlords in the North and the Shia clients of Iran. The warlords went so far as to fly their own flag; they would not display the national flag of Iraq. They also announced that they were going to let contracts for oil exploration in the North (which they did to a Norwegian firm), *and keep the revenue for themselves*—not share with the national government.

Meanwhile, back in the United States, Senator Joseph Biden, running for president, espoused a plan to break Iraq up into three parts—Shia, Kurdish, and Sunni.[74] This was the plan he got from the president emeritus of the Council on Foreign Relations (America's most prestigious private foreign policy institute).

I have never suggested anywhere in this study that the resistance is a national one. I have said that it seemed to be tending toward becoming so. At the same time, I have not discerned any of the resistance groups calling for the return of the Ba'th. What I do see is a genuine fear among native Iraqis that they are losing their country; that the Americans are going to acquiesce in its breakup. Bush has repudiated any such intent, but there does seem to be a drift in this direction.Certainly, were this to happen, it would please the neo-cons, since that would be one less coherent Arab entity Israel would have to deal with.

I believe what is driving the resistance at this point is fear of the Americans' ultimate designs for the country. I do not believe that Moktada, or the ex-officers, and certainly not the whole of the Sunni community, will allow themselves either to be run by an Iranian quisling government or have their country deconstructed along the lines of what has gone on in Palestine. I will have more to say about this in the final/analysis section.

Analysis and Conclusion

Now we have reached the analysis part. My idea throughout this book has been to provide the reader with context; that way he/she might be more willing to accept interpretations which, absent such contextual data, would, I suspect, be rejected.

The main point that I have focused on is the fact of the Iraqis having resisted. To me, there cannot be any question, after surveying events of the invasion phase, that resistance occurred.

Moreover the resistance, although it subsided when the Americans declared victory, certainly flared anew immediately afterward. And I think I have provided ample evidence of what might have triggered the recurrence.

I further provided background on the two previous wars Iraq was involved in, to show that the Iraqis resisted there also. They fought for eight years against Iran, and then, in 1991, against the Americans. Both these wars were vicious. The Iran-Iraq War ended in a victory for Iraq. Conversely, in the first Iraq War—against the Americans—it lost; nonetheless, the Iraqis resisted—the fact of their having stood up to the intense 45-day air bombardment testifies to that.

The second Iraq War is what we have been looking into here, cataloguing the resistance of the Iraqi people and their determination, despite suffering, to preserve their country. This, I recognize, is a subjective view. Others may dispute that there is any kind of organized resistance going on in Iraq; that it is rather pure anarchy. I am not so sure—I think that the revolt, whatever it is, is on the way to developing into something much bigger. Into what? I am not sure that I know.

What was my aim in shaping the book so as to bring out the fact of there having been resistance? I wanted to make the point that the Ba'th was a legitimate regime. There is no greater test of a regime's legitimacy than the people's willingness to fight for it. And this has nothing to do with the character of the regime; I never argued, anywhere in the book, that the Ba'th was benevolent; just that it was legitimate, in the sense that it ruled—it ruled for long and it ruled, I think, fairly broadly, and—good or bad—Iraqis recognized it as their own.

If the regime was legitimate, then the United States and Britain committed a great crime by overthrowing it. However, that is not a matter we need dwell upon. It is an unfortunate fact that empires commit crimes, and there is not much that can be done about it; in a manner of speaking, it is in the nature of things. I was more interested in finding out why the United States handled the occupation so badly. Why, four years on, is this war still having to be waged?

I think the answer is to be found in exploring the nature of the Bush administration. The reader will notice I am shifting the focus of the enquiry now to the United States, away from Iraq. I see no point in further probing the behavior of the Iraqis, which, to me, is self evident: the Iraqis were aggressed against; they fought back—this is normal.

But in the case of the United States, nothing is normal; about America's behavior in this war very little is easily explained. Why, with all of its resources, with all that it has at hand to draw upon, cannot the United States subdue the Iraqis? For the answer to that I think we have to look to the domestic side.

The Republicans came to Washington in 1994 determined they were going to *diss* the Democrats, for all time. I think that was the purpose of the Contract With America (and its offshoot, the K-Street Project).[1] The focus back then was on domestic politics, but subsequently, under Bush, it was expanded into the foreign policy arena. I think that the second Iraq War was something in the nature of a party-building exercise, a way of enlisting support for the Republicans from interests primarily focused overseas.

I think in return for early support for the war, parties tied in with the military/industrial complex got big payoffs. Think Halliburton; think Bechtel. The biggest gainers, however, were the armaments manufacturers. This war, of the United States against Iraq, rejuvenated the arms industry in the United States. After the collapse of the Soviet Union, Congress was disposed to cut appropriations for the military. Speaking metaphorically, one could say that the second Iraq War put the military back on the rails after the Train Wreck of the late 1980s.[2]

But it is important to specify that the war did not have to be against Iraq; in other words, after the fall of the Soviet Union, those Americans who comprised the war party were spoiling for a fight. They wanted to go to war, and it could have been against anybody—it did not need to be Iraq. At the same time a war against the Iraqis had appeal for a number of reasons. First, the Iraqis were debilitated from their ordeal in the first Iraq War and from the ravages of the sanctions. It was expected that they could not defend themselves. Along with that, the neo-cons had been agitating for a war against Iraq for some time. Hence, they were set to go (after 9/11), with arguments to show why the Iraqis should be made the enemy. And most influential perhaps was the fact of Iraq being saddled with a rogue nation-reputation—a feature of the Americans' prejudicial regard, discussed in the third chapter. Not a lot of promotional work had to be done: people could relate to the idea of going to war with Iraq—*a bad nation*. Finally a war against an Arab state held out hope, for the Republicans, of capturing the Jewish vote, something the Democrats are supposed to have sewn up.

But if that was the main aim of Bush—to aggrandize the Republican party by inciting a war for which there would be payoffs—what does that tell us about the spirit in which the war was undertaken? *I do not think that Bush ever took it seriously.* Once the war was a go, so to speak, once the payoffs started coming in, Bush effectively washed his hands of it. It then became Rumsfeld's baby; the actual carrying out of the war was left to the defense secretary.

Rumsfeld was a true believer, committed to revolutionizing the way that America fights wars. At the same time it is not as though he was not under compulsion to do as he was doing. In the United States, producing weapons is a business—not a private enterprise-type business, because the arms industry is largely government funded. It is rather something on the order of a social works project. Arms production provides jobs in states where arms factories are located; it produces ancillary businesses, spin-offs like electronics, and software, industries grown out of government-funded research.

Along with this, selling weapons overseas is a big, *big* money maker for the United States. It is not generally recognized but, before the first Iraq War, the Gulf sheikhs were the mainstay of America's military/industrial complex, so many sophisticated weapons systems did they purchase.

However, the weapons *systems*—such big money makers for the manu-facturers—*were designed to be wielded against a superpower,* like the Soviet Union, and when the Soviets collapsed the rationale for their continued production disappeared.

Rumsfeld's task was to find a way of justifying the future production of arms, a way which would convince Congress they were yet useful and necessary. In the Afghan War, Rumsfeld went all out targeting the Taliban with stealth bombers and all of the most lethal, sophisticated weapons in America's arsenal. And at the end of that war, it seemed he had licked the problem: he could justify using all of this high-tech weaponry because, so lethal was it, nothing apparently could withstand it. Wars could be gotten over with fast and without any great expenditure.

In other words, because you had all of this sophisticated stuff, you could fight wars cheaply. You did not have to commit huge ground forces, as America did in the first Iraq War, a terribly expensive proposition.

You could unleash the air war strategy, and, as happened in the Afghan War, the enemy would lay down practically at once, unable to resist the awfulness of the war's impact.

Wars in the era of Shock and Awe would become no big deal. So quickly could they be gotten over, and with so little expense, no one (in the United States) would think twice about waging them.

The problem, however, as we have now come to see, is that the air war strategy does not always work. Air wars can be successful, but only where certain conditions obtain. In Afghanistan the Americans were dealing with a tribal society, and, as I have pointed out elsewhere,[3] tribalists never—or at least rarely ever—go the limit in waging war. Ultimately, against too great odds, they decamp; they flee to the mountains, or into the outback where they can regroup to return and fight another day. They will never quixotically elect to die fighting. So one can expect to be able to bomb them into submission; as occurred.

The same does not apply to mature nation/states, which I think Iraq was on the verge of becoming when the Iran-Iraq War ended in 1988. Under such setups, the citizenry, if reasonably satisfied with their lot, are more likely to fight to preserve that which they value. Of course prior to the second Iraq War, the received wisdom in the United States was that the Iraqis *were not* satisfied; they supposedly were yearning to be free of the regime of Saddam Hussein and of the Ba'thists. But that was a view promoted by the neo-cons, on the basis of no accurate knowledge of conditions in Iraq.

There were, to be sure, experts in the United States who could have informed the administration as to the true condition; who could have counseled caution, as Iraq was unlikely to be the pushover the neo-cons were predicting; but they never got a chance to register their objections. Perle, Wolfowitz, Feith, the people around Rumfeld, squelched all dissent.[4] As a result, no debate on the war was conducted. That is why, I say, Bush never took the war seriously. He accepted the misinformed opinions of the neo-cons without ever thinking to solicit alternate views; he embarked on the war as if it were to be a "cake walk." And with Rumsfeld in charge of waging the war—Rumsfeld, who, as I say, was committed to the proposition that wars could be waged predominantly from the air—it is no wonder that complications developed. It quickly became apparent that, up against an enemy like Iraq—that is, one determined to fight—many more ground troops were needed.

So why, then, did the Americans not lay on more troops, to overwhelm the Iraqi resistance and crush it before it had a chance to set down roots, getting itself established? The answer that is out there, as we say, is that this would have entailed reinstituting the draft, and the Bush administration did not believe it could put that one over.

I doubt this. Whatever else one wants to say about the Bush administration, under Karl Rove's guidance, it showed itself willing *and able* to market practically anything. Rove is the premier operator in this department. Take the fact of Bush's having been willing to "reform" Social Security. This is supposed to be the third rail of American politics, but the administration essayed to overhaul it. If it was willing to tilt against Social Security, who is to say it could not have made a fight over the draft?

I think the reason why it did not was that Bush saw no need. The interests for whom the president had initiated the war were not complaining. Over the course of it, the fortunes of the defense contractors had turned completely around: they are now making money hand over fist.[5] And what about Big Oil? It appears the American-sponsored government in Iraq is set to pass (as of this writing) legislation to invite back the major oil companies, giving them lucrative contracts, guaranteeing a percentage of profits no other country has ever assigned them.[6] Israel's supporters are not perturbed. If Iraq disappears as a formal entity; if millions of Iraqis are rendered stateless; Israel will yet be well served: one less coherent Arab foe to worry about.[7]

In a manner of speaking there was no feedback loop operating here. No one who had an "in" with the Bush administration was concerned about the way things were going.[8] Hence no correction. As long as Bush's main constituents, the big contributors, were happy, he felt under no compulsion to change course. For the special interests, starting the war was enough; winning it would be nice, but not necessary. Take for example the defense contractors—win or lose, the government is going to be buying lots more weapons forever—if the war party has its way.

Whereas the outcome of the elections certainly signaled that a course correction was necessary, there is no evidence that Bush was aware of this before the elections came off. Had he been, he would have fired Rumsfeld before, not after the Republicans were savaged at the polls.

One more argument in favor of my theory that the war was politically motivated is that which happened with the so-called reconstruction. Whom did Bush send out to do the work of building Iraq back up, once it became apparent the country could not function, so blasted was it? Party hacks. Youths whose only recommendation was that they had worked for the Republicans and so were due a payoff.[9]

Throughout the planning and execution of the war, Bush and his team exhibited a fine disregard for consequences. Which, to me, says that they were not taking the thing seriously.

Now, to conclude, I want to look at where the war is going, and this will involve a consideration of geopolitics. Essentially there have been three eras of what I would call Anglo-Saxon domination in the Middle East. The first was from World War I until 1969, where Britain was the hegemon operating in collusion with Big Oil, and, there, control was exercised through the oil contracts. By procuring deals with the potentates, the oil companies were able to trade protection (for the potentates) for hard cash.

That era ended with the OPEC Revolution (in 1973) when the oil producers winkled the companies out of their contracts and took control of their own resources. But—and this important—*the potentates allowed the companies to share.* Essentially a few big (British and American) companies continued drawing huge profits as traders for the oil producers. And to ensure the perpetuation of this arrangement, the United States took on the job of keeping the potentates in power. Here, control was exercised through the military agreements.[10]

The second era ended in 1988 with the initiation of the collapse of the Soviet Union. The United States and the potentates had been justifying their collusion on the basis of the Gulf having to be guarded against Soviet penetration. The potentates could sell that to their people because communism, an avowedly atheistic doctrine, was perceived by Muslims as a threat to Islam. (A more direct threat could hardly be imagined because the Gulf, along with being the locus of all that oil wealth, is also the site of Islam's holiest places.) However, once the Soviet Union went under that rationale was no longer effective.

With that, the Americans, the Israelis, the Egyptians, the oil sheikhs and the Pakistanis (but not the Iranians, because the Shah of Iran had been overthrown by this time) attempted to keep up the old Cold War network of alliances by claiming the new threat was the Islamic Republic. It was fear of Khomeiniism spreading to Afghanistan and throughout the Gulf that led the Saudis to finance the CIA-sponsored *mujahadeen* movement and motivated the United States to support Iraq's war against Iran up until 1985, when—with Iran/Contra—Washington switched to backing the mullahs. The reason Washington switched was it perceived Baghdad on the point of winning its fight. The Americans never intended that Baghdad should become a regional power in the Persian Gulf; that could not be, not if America intended to hold on to its hegemony in this so strategic part of the world.

Egypt, Israel, Pakistan, and the Saudis and the rest of the Gulf sheikhs then joined the United States in promoting the war of democracy against terror, which found a new foe in Osama bin Laden, the supposed mastermind of a movement of Sunni Muslim radicals bent on destroying the West.

However, what ought to have been a concomitant of the Terror War, that the Middle Easterners could expect to be lifted out of their wretched economic condition, never materialized. And it did not because all Washington really ever was interested in was maintaining its alliance network of client regimes, a system underpinned by the defense contracts. The rulers enter into these arms deals because they profit from them, in the form of commissions on the contracts (i.e., bribes).[11]

The problem for America was that, with the exception of Israel, none of these regimes is legitimate because their people all are disaffected. The regimes in Egypt, Pakistan, Saudi Arabia, and the Gulf sheikhdoms are all viewed by their people as corrupt, composed, in most instances, of military castes. The castes look to perpetuate their rule, and have no thought for the welfare of their people.

What is the one area that the so-called Islamic movement focuses on to draw recruits? Welfare. The people go to Hizbollah in Lebanon, to Hamas in Palestine, to the Muslim Brotherhood in Egypt, to have their basic needs attended to, which the castes will not look out for because their bureaucracies are indifferent, and consequently inept.

The Americans maintain that welfare funding comes from Iran, and also from wealthy sheikhs who contribute to Muslim charities unaware that their contributions fund terror. I do not think that is true. There may be some of this, but in fact it is a long-standing pattern in the Middle East for the religious to provide welfare when governments fail. The governments prove derelict, and the people, needing to be taken care of, turn to the religious. In that sense one can say the growth of fundamentalism, far from being a proactive conspiracy, actually derives from the failure of the states.

So what is the problem? Let these corrupt regimes flounder; that is no concern of the United States, is it? Well it is, certainly—because of the oil. The area where all of the unrest is bubbling up is the Persian Gulf, where 60 percent of the world's proven oil supplies are located. America cannot claim to be the hegemon, if it cannot secure the Gulf. And this brings us back to the problem of how America fights wars.

As I said above, the air war strategy does not always work. One reason it does not is that the Middle East is awash with weapons. As long as determined guerrillas can lay their hands on means to resist, they will. And, as we have seen in the most recent case of resistance (against the Israelis in Lebanon), the guerrillas often are able to defend themselves with some competency.

The advent of missile technology (in 1973) revolutionized the conduct of war in the Middle East. In that war—between the Arabs and Israel—the Arabs wielded missiles to keep the Israelis at bay, and for a time they were successful at it. If the United States had not intervened, the Arabs might have achieved their objectives in the conflict.

But now the development of arms technology has undergone a further advance: we now have cheap remote detonating devices. And these, because they are easy to acquire and to maintain—and are terribly lethal in their effects—enable non-state actors, like Hizbollah in Lebanon and the Iraqi insurgents, to wreak awful devastation, even on sophisticated militaries like that of Israel and the United States.

We are certainly seeing it now in Iraq where the insurgency has developed the use of improvised explosive devices to a high art.

Now, is it likely that the United States will adapt its tactics to compensate for this new development? Will it abandon the air war strategy? Or even modify it, so as to engage the paramilitaries? I do not think so. To overcome guerrillas, modern armies must be willing to occupy areas the guerrillas hold—to clear them out. That means infantry-heavy forces, and for reasons I have just elaborated, the United States cannot fight a war on that basis without incurring significant severe dislocation on the home front.

Effectively, then, the conduct of war by the United States—and this also is the case with Israel—has become retributive. The armies of both wreak vengeance on their adversaries. "If you can't beat 'em, hurt 'em," seems to be the operational theory. The proponents of the air war strategy may believe that in this way they ultimately will prevail: inflict such destruction on the enemy that he finally will succumb. But it has not worked out that way. Just as with the Vietnamese, it very much does appear Middle Easterners have an infinite capacity for absorbing pain.

Moreover, the non-state actors have begun exacting retribution on their part. In this regard, the appearance of suicide bombers is a dreadful innovation. The Muslims have invoked an escalating spiral of destruction— on themselves as well as their enemies. This type of warfare is irrational, but that does not seem to stop it from occurring.

If the United States and Israel keep on the way they are going, one very much fears they will reduce the Middle East to a wasteland. Look at what happened most recently in Lebanon. There, *what you saw was what you got.* The Israelis may have claimed they were out to destroy Hizbollah, but I seriously doubt that they ever entertained such a possibility. I think their aim was rather to degrade Lebanon's infrastructure. Israel deliberately set out to crater roads, blow up bridges, destroy electric grids—in a phrase, to do as James Baker so graphically put it, bomb the country back to the Stone Age.[12] In the last two days of the war—*after the cease-fire was agreed upon*—Israel, according to the United Nations, dropped several million cluster bombs on the southern Shia area of the country. Why, if not to kill civilians?[13]

Similarly, the United States has trashed Iraq. The casualty toll among Iraqis is appalling. The Lancet Report claims as many as 600,000 may have been inflicted.[14] And, of course, what infrastructure Iraq possessed now has been destroyed. It is not likely that Iraq will ever come back, just as it may be the case that Lebanon will never recover.

But why do not the Arabs—the Palestinians, the Lebanese, the Iraqis— capitulate? Do they not know that they face certain defeat? *Sure, but what is the alternative for them?* Helotage. Without any reciprocity on offer from the Americans, there is no incentive for them to get in line. For all of their talk about the benefits of democracy-to-come, the Americans have not announced any large-scale rebuilding schemes; there is no Marshall Plan for the Middle East in the works, as far as I am aware. Rather, the neo-cons believe the free enterprise system, left to work itself out, will raise all boats, as we say.

My belief is that the Bush administration's reliance on the free enterprise system is disingenuous. I think that the policy makers, in Israel as well as the United States, are banking on the Arabs' complete submission. This is the Likud strategy, which Cheney certainly, and maybe Bush, has bought into. The Likudniks envision turning the area back to the condition of the 1950s, when the whole of the Arab world was in a client relationship with Britain and the United States.[15] I do not think the Arabs—considering all that has transpired in the area since the 1950s—will acquiesce to this.

There is a final irony involved here. In years past, the United States (and before it Britain) was able to control the Middle East *indirectly*. It did it by putting in place two ingenious schemes. The first was the international oil system, whereby control was achieved through negotiating oil contracts. Then there was the arms transfer system, and here the control mechanism was the arms agreement. In both instances, the United States and Britain obtained a usufruct, which, once they had it, precluded their having to actually possess the oil.

The arms transfer system was particularly ingenious. The Americans bought oil from the potentates. The sheikhs then returned petro dollars to the Americans—much of it through arms purchases. And, as I mentioned above, a part of the payment was returned to the sheikhs in the form of commissions (bribes), and a part of that the sheikhs doled out to their retainers. That way a network was built up of individuals in the Gulf whose lifestyles depended on keeping in with the Americans.

Unfortunately, however, there was a flaw in this arrangement: leakage. That is, the weapons got passed to parties outside the system. A potential leak came about in the late 1970s, with the fall of the Shah. The Shah bought sophisticated weapons systems he could not possibly use because his army, being composed of uneducated peasants, was incapable of manipulating them. (When this was pointed out to Nixon and Kissinger by concerned officers at the Pentagon, Kissinger is supposed to have opined: all the better; if he cannot use them, he cannot get in trouble with them.)

But then the Shah was overthrown and the weapons fell into the hands of the Khomeiniists. This should have constituted a great catastrophe for the Americans. However, as I noted above, Khomeini disdained the Shah's modern army, seen as a vehicle of corruption. So he gutted it. The Revolutionary Guards, who then made up the new army of the Islamic Republic, they, too, being uneducated, could not use the weapons. Hence, the development of the human wave attack, to compensate for this lack.

Effectively, then, leakage which might have occurred over the fall of the Shah and appearance of Khomeini was stanched, purely as luck would have it. But then came the Iran-Iraq War. For a time, the Ba'thists were able to fund arms purchases on their own. But once the war turned against them (in 1982) they quickly ran out of cash. At which point, the Gulf sheikhs—fearing the spread of Khomeiniism—undertook to equip them: Saudi

Arabia, Kuwait and the UAE bought enormous amounts of weapons—of all kinds—which they supplied to the Iraqis. (Weapons in such great quantity and of such lethality were needed, because Iraq, outnumbered three to one by the Iranians, had to rely on overwhelming firepower to keep the Islamic Republic at bay.) In any event, for the military/industrial complex these were truly the bonanza years, when it very much appeared the money would never stop flowing.

However, unlike the case with Iran, the Iraqis did not merely acquire the weapons; they made sure they could use them. In this, the Ba'thists were advantaged by having pushed universal literacy and education up to the college level in Iraq, so the Iraqis were not uneducated peasants, as had been the case with Shah's army. Moreover, the Iraqis, as I said above, inveigled the Americans into tutoring them, not just in how to perform with the arms; they strove to grasp the principle of modern warfare. Before they were done, I have it on the authority of American attaches who served there, the Iraqis had absorbed the techniques of combined arms.

It is now the case that these weapons, which Hussein acquired in such great quantities, are in the hands of the ex-army officers, who are able to wield them; furthermore, since they know how the Americans fight wars, they are also enabled to adopt measures to defeat the U.S. military's counterinsurgency efforts.

There is the irony: the system the Americans worked out—the arms transfer system, meant to keep control of the oil—is now working to undermine hegemony. The transfer problem—namely, the tendency of transferred weapons to bleed out of the system—is real. Disaffected populations in the Middle East now have the means whereby to attack the castes which for so long have neglected them, and, by weakening them, they raise the specter of breaching America's alliance network.

Sooner or later, I think it is reasonable to assume, one of the surviving clients of the United States is going to be overthrown (as happened with the Shah) and then it will hemorrhage weapons, and I very much doubt that the United States will be able to contain the effects of that disgorgement.

At the same time, I do not see any sign that anyone in Washington, or in Tel Aviv, or in London, is giving a thought to this possibility. The same imprudent disregard for consequences that led America into the disastrous war with Iraq seems to be operating still as the United States pursues its involvement in the area.

Notes

INTRODUCTION

1. I hesitate to give a figure of how many casualties there were, for the reason that both sides in the war were closed societies which never gave out statistics on anything, much less the number of casualties they experienced in a war. I have seen figures claiming the war cost up to a million and half dead, both sides. I find that hard to believe, but certainly the war was a bloody one.

2. To be sure the Iraqis and Iranians were not fighting each other as such. Since there was no such thing as a state of Iraq until after the first World War, they could not have been. But all the centuries when the Turkish and Iranian empires confronted each other, the people living in Iraq (then called Mesopotamia) fought for the Turks against the legions of the then-Shahs.

3. These are the criteria laid out by George Bush for any government he would deem successful in Iraq. See "Bush Faces Battery of Ugly Choices on War Tactics, if Not on Strategy," *New York Times,* October 20, 2006.

CHAPTER 1

1. "U.S. Is Pressing for Turks' Help in Move on Iraq," *New York Times,* November 28, 2002.

2. Actually there was more to it than this. During the first Iraq War, Turkey's then-prime minister Turgut Ozal supported the U.S. effort to eject Iraq from Kuwait, to the extent of allowing the Americans to use Incirlik air base as a launching pad for raids on Iraq. He did this over the objections of not just the Turkish people but the Turkish military as well. Ozal insisted that Turkey, by allying itself with the United States, would reap economic benefits in the aftermath of the war. Ozal's claims conflicted with Turkey's situation at the time, where the economy was experiencing a marked improvement as Iraq, Turkey, and Iran had inaugurated a regional trading bloc. In fact no economic benefits flowed to Turkey once the war had ended; indeed the economy experienced a sharp slowdown. So angered and disillusioned were the

Turks over this that they voted Ozal out of office. Turkey was then led successively by the Republican People's Party (RPP) and Justice Party, tenures marked by continuing bad economic performance and corruption. It was then that the previously banned Islamic party won election, but the Turkish military intervened to try and deny Erdogan the prime minister position because of an attack he had made on Turkey's policy of secularism, a criminal offense in Turkey. And, of course, Turkey's unwillingness to support a war against Iraq was fueled also by the Turks' attitudes towards the Kurds, which I will go into below.

3. "Disappointed Wolfowitz Still Supports U.S.-Turkish Defense Ties," *American Armed Forces Information Services,* May 7, 2003. In this Pentagon interview with CNN, Wolfowitz said that whereas he still supports strong ties between the United States and Turkey, he nonetheless was "disappointed" with the Turks over their refusal to allow the planned U.S. invasion of Iraq from Turkey to go ahead. The Turkish government "for whatever reasons," he said, "was prepared to make it difficult for the Iraqi people to be liberated, was prepared seemingly to deal with one of the worst dictators—somebody who probably killed millions of Muslims."

4. Indeed, the Fourth arrived too late to take an active part in the war.

5. "A Swift, and Risky, Attack by Land, with Surprise in Mind," *New York Times,* March 21, 2003.

6. "Strikes Intensify as Forces Move North," *Washington Post,* March 22, 2003.

7. Michael Gordon and General Bernard Trainor, *Cobra II* (New York: Pantheon Books, 2006). In *New York Times* military correspondent Michael Gordon's account of the war, a number of possible explanations for Franks's switch are investigated. Some are plausible, some are not. However, the actual reason Franks gave, that, to me, remains unconvincing.

8. This was one of the misapprehensions of the Americans, that the Iraqis believed that there might be a reprieve. The Iraqis knew that the Bush administration had its heart set on invading and occupying Iraq, and that nothing was going to prevent that from happening; so it was never a question of "if (with the Iraqis)." They expected the attack to come when it came; the matter was never in doubt.

9. "A Swift, and Risky, Attack by Land, with Surprise in Mind."

10. That there was some basis for this fear can be seen from the following. Opponents of the war were able to make considerable capital out of the fact that the only site in Baghdad the Americans protected was the oil ministry, while they allowed other important sites—including the national museum, repository of priceless artifacts—to be looted.

11. Makiya wrote a book, *Republic of Fear* (New York, NY: Pantheon Books, 1989), under a pseudonym, Samir al Khalil. Riddled with errors, many of them—it would appear to me—meant to be deliberately misleading; the book resembled what journalists back in the 1960s (when I was one) called a hatchet job. The book was widely quoted by the neo-cons, who cited its misinformation in many of their appeals for America to go to war with Iraq.

12. Actually it probably would be more correct to say Rumsfeld espoused the Revolution in Military Affairs (RMA) doctrine of Pentagon strategist Andy Marshall. The RMA was being touted just before the second Iraq War. Briefly, the idea was, anything you do with ground troops (bodies) you could do better, cheaper,

and more efficiently with machines. We at the U.S. Army War College, when I was a professor there, could only wonder at such far out ideas as this.

13. For a comparison of Powell's kind of war and Rumsfeld's, see "Calibrated War Makes a Comeback," *Washington Post,* March 21, 2003. Powell's type of war was also what Eisenhower advocated.

14. For the effort of the generals to slow things down see Thomas Ricks, *Fiasco* (New York: Penguin Press, 2006).

15. A similar instance where those conducting a major military operation seemed to be willing victory, as they evinced no method in their performance, was World War I, with the British High Command at Passchendaele. See Robin Prior and Trevor Wilson, *Passechendaele, the Untold Story* (New Haven, CT: Yale University Press, 1996), 172.

16. These are all substantial cities, with populations in the hundreds of thousands; Nasiriyah is a half a million.

17. "U.S. Forces at Edge of Blacked-Out Baghdad," *New York Times,* April 4, 2003.

18. "Bombarding Baghdad, Deaths in Battle, and Rising Support for Bush," *New York Times,* March 22, 2003.

19. "The Blitz Over Baghdad," *New York Times,* March 22, 2003.

20. Hussein, in a manner of speaking, left the regulars out to dry. At the end of the war, when the Americans were obviously winning, Hussein pulled his elite units back from Kuwait into Iraq—for the last defense, evidently—while leaving the regular army units pretty much to fend for themselves, and several were badly shot up by the Americans.

21. The Guards play a significant role in the resistance, and I will have more to say about them in the next chapter.

22. Gordon and Trainor, *Cobra II.* According to Gordon, Bush stressed to American commanders leading the attack that they were to play up three things: photos of joyful Iraqis greeting the American "liberation," pictures of American humanitarian relief getting through to the Iraqis, and pictures of captured WMD. Obviously none of these things panned out.

23. "The Blitz Over Baghdad."

24. "Rumsfeld's Imperious Style Turns Combative," *New York Times,* March 30, 2003.

25. "Military Leaves Reputation for Caution in the Dust," *Washington Post,* March 22, 2003.

26. Ibid.

27. "Heavy Iraqi Losses Seen in Big Battle," *New York Times,* March 26, 2003.

28. Ibid.

29. "British See Uprising Civilians in Basra" [*sic*], *Washington Post,* March 26, 2003.

30. "New Iraqi Force Emerges," *New York Times,* March 24, 2003.

31. To give Franks his due, there was some hype. Reporters were claiming that some of these Fedayeen were going into battle wearing white (death) shrouds. I doubt that. "Lowering Expectations," *New York Times,* March 24, 2003.

32. "Troops Advance Halfway to Baghdad," *Washington Post,* March 23, 2003.

33. "'One Good Fight, But Little Else,'" *Washington Post,* March 23, 2003.

34. Bob Woodward, *State of Denial* (New York: Simon & Schuster, 2006).

35. "Marines, Battling in Streets, Seek Control of City in the South," *New York Times,* March 25, 2003.

36. See "Rumsfeld's Imperious Style Turns Combative," *New York Times,* March 30, 2003, for a discussion of Rumsfeld's propensity to lose his cool under pressure.

37. "U.S. Acts to Shore Up Supply Lines; Units Advancing on Baghdad Reported to be Short of Fuel," *Washington Post,* March 26, 2003.

38. There was another reason it was essential to cross the Euphrates: the Americans had to have troops positioned along the Iran-Iraq border to prevent incursions by the Iranians.

39. "Troops Advance Halfway to Baghdad," *Washington Post,* March 23, 2003.

40. "Iraq Violates Rules of War," March 24, 2003.

41. If you read over other firsthand accounts of Americans who fought, this reaction repeats quite frequently.

42. See Tim Pritchard, *Ambush Alley* (New York: Ballentine Books, 2007).

43. "Rumsfeld Faulted for Troop Dilution," *Washington Post,* March 30, 2003.

44. "U.S. Shifting Focus of Land Campaign to Fight in South," *New York Times,* March 26, 2003.

45. Pritchard, *Ambush Alley,* 103. Also see Trish Woods, *What Was Asked of Us, An Oral History of the Iraq War by the Soldiers Who Fought It* (New York: Little Brown & Co., 2006).

46. Evidence that these were Republican Guards appears in *What Was Asked of Us,* where one of the Marines, describing the battle of Nasiriyah, comments that the Fedayeen (he says) were distinguished by having a small red triangle on their sleeves. The red triangle is the insignia of the Guards.

47. People like Ahmed Chalabi, about whom I will have a great deal more to say below.

48. "Iraq's Outside-In Strategy More Effective than Anticipated," *Washington Post,* March 28, 2003.

49. Interestingly, compared to the first Iraq War, there were not many of these. In the first war, 50,000, as compared with 6,000 in this.

50. "With Bombing, Iraqis Escalate Tactics and Show New Danger in Front Lines," *New York Times,* March 30, 2003.

51. "Allies Struggle for Supply Lines," *Washington Post,* March 30, 2003.

52. The description, as to the composition of the Fedayeen, changed over the course of the war. Later, it was claimed that the Fedayeen, estimated to comprise as many as 60,000 irregulars, actually were led by commanders of the elite Republican Guard. Later that was amended to say that Republican Guardsmen and *Mukhabarat* (security) officers too were fighting in these units. Corroboration for my theory that Fedayeen was a made up name is the fact that the Ba'thists never referred to them. They said that irregulars were opposing the Americans but never identified them specifically as Saddam's Fedayeen. Also, after the war, when the resistance developed, many groups sprang up claiming to be resistance fighters. None ever called itself Saddam's Fedayeen. If, as the Americans said, this was the outfit

that was doing most of the fighting, one would think it would have carried on after the war.

53. Tim Pritchard, "When Iraq Went Wrong," *New York Times,* December 6, 2006.

54. "Iraqi Defiance Renews Debate Over Air Power; War Experts Differ on Effectiveness of Coalition Strategy," *Washington Post,* March 29, 2003.

55. Ibid.

56. Ibid.

57. "Allies Struggle For Supply Lines," *Washington Post,* March 30, 2003.

58. "Blasts in Baghdad, *New York Times,* March 27, 2003.

59. Ibid.

60. "Military Defends Risk of Aggressive Tactics," *New York Times,* April 9, 2003.

61. "Rumsfeld Insists War Plan Is Sound," *Washington Post,* March 29, 2003.

62. "Rumsfeld Design for War Criticized on the Battlefield," *New York Times,* April 1, 2003.

63. Gordon and Trainor, *Cobra II.*

64. See Jacquline De Romilly, *The Rise and Fall of States According to Greek Authors* (Ann Arbor: The University of Michigan Press, 1977), 58 for a discussion of the ancient Greeks' understanding of hubris.

65. "Allies Confront Baghdad Defenders; Iraqis Repel Copters; One Goes Down," *New York Times,* March 25, 2003.

66. "Heavy Iraqi Losses Seen in Big Battle," *New York Times,* March 26, 2003.

67. "Allied Air and Ground Units Try to Weaken Baath Party's Grip," *New York Times,* March 30, 2003.

68. "Iraq Says Market Blast Kills 58," *Washington Post,* March 29, 2003.

69. What somewhat contradicts this is the fact of the initial Fedayeen fighters wearing that curious black garb, which would seem to indicate a formal outfit. But this might have been misconstrued. Just as Third World fighters—as I noted elsewhere—adopted the style and modus operandi of the African technicals, so the pattern of wearing a peculiar form of dress became the vogue with them also. To wear black sweat suits was the mark of the urban guerrilla. It goes back as far as the Palestinian attack on the Israeli athletes at the Olympics.

70. "Suicide Bombing Kills 4 Soldiers," *Washington Post,* March 30, 2003.

71. "Iraq Violates Rules of War, U.S. Complains," *New York Times,* March 24, 2003.

72. Ibid.

73. "Standoff in Basrah Hints at Tough Time in Baghdad," *Washington Post,* March 30, 2003.

74. "Army Has Its First Close Clash with Republican Guard Units," *Washington Post,* April 1, 2003; and "Allies Widen Hold on Iraq, Civil Strife on Rise," *New York Times,* April 11, 2003.

75. "U.S. Losses Light as Iraqi Toll Surges in Baghdad Fighting," *Washington Post,* April 8, 2003.

76. Ibid.

77. Ibid.

78. "Allies and Iraqis Battle on 2 Fronts; 20 Americans Dead or Missing; 50 Hurt," *New York Times,* March 24, 2003.

79. Of course, the Muslims do not have saints. But, if they had them, Ali, the son-in-law of the Prophet, would rank very high up in the Pantheon, at least of the Shias.

80. It is obvious that, after Rumsfeld performed his strategy shift, and began attrition bombing, it was the Iraqi army and most particularly the Republican Guard units he was going after. The record is replete with statements to this effect by American commanders, and also with claims that the Guards had been decimated. Given this state of affairs, it is seemingly contradictory, the Americans' claim that the Guard did not fight. More on this below. For statements, by Americans, of devastation wreaked on the Guard see, "'Good Progress' So Far; Worse May Lie Ahead," *New York Times,* April 1, 2003; "2 U.S. Columns Are Advancing on Baghdad Defenses," *New York Times,* April 1, 2003; "Iraq Is Planning Protracted War," *New York Times,* April 2, 2003; "Goal of U.S.: Avoid a Seige," *New York Times,* April 3, 2003; "Aerial Pounding Intended to Push Iraq's Government Toward Brink," *New York Times,* March 21, 2003; and "U.S. Shifting Focus of Land Campaign to Fight in South," *New York Times,* March 25, 2003.

81. "A Tightening of the Noose," *New York Times,* April 4, 2003.

82. "A Show of Force," *New York Times,* April 6, 2003.

83. "Hussein Fate after Attack Still Unclear," *New York Times,* April 9, 2003.

84. "In Shift, Air War Targets Communications Facilities," *Washington Post,* April 1, 2003.

85. "Unfolding Battle Will Determine Length of War," *Washington Post,* March 25, 2003.

86. Ibid.

87. "U.S. Forces Seize 2 Hussein Palaces as Armor Reaches Heart of Baghdad," *Washington Post,* April 8, 2003.

88. "In Iraqi Capital, Sirens Proceed Two Direct Hits," *New York Times,* March 21, 2003.

89. "Iraq's Outside-In Strategy More Effective Than Anticipated."

90. "Iraq Is Planning Protracted War," *New York Times,* April 2, 2003.

91. "Standoff at Basrah Hints at Tough Time in Baghdad," *Washington Post,* March 30, 2003.

92. "Casualties Stoke Hostility Over British Presence," *Washington Post,* April 9, 2003.

93. "A Show of Force," *New York Times,* April 6, 2003.

94. "Baghdad Falls, Though Fighting Persists," *New York Times,* April 8, 2003.

95. "Army Has First Close Clashes with Republican Guard Units," *Washington Post,* April 1, 2003.

96. "Guards, Irregulars Take Up Positions," *Washington Post,* April 6, 2003.

97. "U.S. Forces at Edge of Blacked-Out Baghdad," *New York Times,* April 4, 2003.

98. "Battalion Stages Assault on Iraqi Hilltop Position and Guard's Complex," *New York Times,* April 9, 2003.

99. These assertions developed later on when L. Paul Bremer III, the Americans' proconsul, sought to defend his decision to disband the Iraqi Army. He claimed the army did not exist, because it had disintegrated before the war was over.

100. For stories of Iraqi resistance see "U.S. Forces Probing Inside Baghdad," *Washington Post,* April 5, 2003; "Overnight a Capital Transformed; Guards, Irregulars Take Up Positions," *Washington Post,* April 6, 2003; "U.S. Forces Seize 2 Hussein Palaces as Armor Reaches Heart of Baghdad," *Washington Post,* April 8, 2003; "U.S. Losses Light as Iraqi Toll Surges in Baghdad Fighting," *Washington Post,* April 8, 2003; "Military Defends Risk of Aggressive Tactics," *Washington Post,* April 9, 2003; "Capital Has Look of a Battlefield," *New York Times,* April 8, 2003; "U.S. Tightens Grip; Rockets Rain on Baghdad," *New York Times,* April 9, 2003; "Key Section of City Is Taken in a Street-by-Street Fight," *New York Times,* April 9, 2003; "Push to Finish Job," *New York Times,* April 9, 2003; "U.S. Forces Take Control in Baghdad, Bush Elated; Some Resistance Remains," *New York Times,* April 10, 2003; "Last Symbol; Tikrit Capture," *New York Times,* April 13, 2003; "Heavy Fighting for Desert Base at Syria Border," *New York Times,* April 11, 2003; "Baghdad Air War Shifts, With G.I.'s in the City," *New York Times,* April 6, 2003; "Urban War Begins; 'It Was Real Scary,'" *New York Times,* April 6, 2003; and "Marines Cruising to Baghdad," *New York Times,* April 4, 2003.

101. "For Weary U.S. Troops, End Is Still Elusive," *New York Times,* April 5, 2003.

102. "Excerpts From Bush's Speech to Veterans Group at the White House, *New York Times,* March 29, 2003.

103. "Iraq Says Tactic to Become Routine Against U.S. Troops," *Washington Post,* March 30, 2003.

CHAPTER 2

1. The belief that Iraq was a satellite of the Soviet Union came in the first years of the new republican government when Qasem (see below) bought arms from the Russians, and later the Iraqis, under the Ba'th (see below), signed a friendship pact with Moscow. At the same time both Qasem and Saddam Hussein, later when he became president, were careful to elude a too stifling embrace of the Soviets, and Hussein at one point carried out an extensive purge of the Iraqi Communists. The irony, however, is that none of this, as we say, cut any ice with the Americans. For a discussion of how Ronald Reagan routinely characterized nationalist Third World governments as proxies of the Soviet Union see Mahmood Mamdani, *Good Muslims, Bad Muslims* (New York: Pantheon Books, 2004), 12.

2. Britain could get away with this because the way the mandate worked, Iraq was practically a colony of the British. Further, Faisal was not an Iraqi: the British had plucked him out of the Hejaz (Saudi Arabia) and installed him as king of Iraq. He had no independent power base and so was entirely dependent on the British. See George Lenczowski, *The Middle East in World Affairs* (Ithaca, NY: Cornell University Press, 1984).

3. After World War I when the Allies broke up the old Ottoman Empire, which had sided with the Central Powers, Britain got the mandate for the newly created territory of Iraq. Britain's ostensible role was that of mentor to prepare the Iraqis

for statehood, actually the British exploited the arrangement to acquire a lockhold on Iraq's oil.

4. Although the British acquiesced in the granting of independence to Iraq, they stayed on in the country, operating behind the scenes. Iraq was, until the time the monarchy was overthrown, a member of the British commonwealth.

5. Gerald De Gaury, *Three Kings in Baghdad* (London: Hutchinson, 1961), 89.

6. Phebe Marr, *The Modern History of Iraq* (Boulder, CO: Westview Press, 1988), 11.

7. Marr, *The Modern History of Iraq,* 57.

8. Marr, *The Modern History of Iraq,* 82.

9. Britain's principal access to oil at this time was through the British Petroleum Company's (BP) concession in Iran, and, in Iraq, the concessions held by the Iraq Petroleum Company (IPC), in which BP and Royal Dutch/Shell participated along with two American companies.

10. For the Baghdad Pact see George Lenczowski, *The Middle East in World Affairs.*

11. De Gaury, *Three Kings in Baghdad,* 195.

12. The Iraqi army was one of the few institutions through which a relatively uneducated Iraqi could move up the scale and improve his status. Prior to the class in which Qasem was enrolled, no educational requirement existed for the military academy. Qasem had a secondary school education, and that was considered exceptional. Members of the Iraqi upper classes disdained to join the army. Hence, the openings for lower class youths.

13. In Egypt, the so-called Free Officers, who led the coup, put Farouk aboard his yacht and allowed him to sail away to exile on the French Riviera.

14. William Eagleton, Jr., *The Kurdish Republic of 1946* (Oxford: Oxford University Press, 1963), 9.

15. Hanna Batatu, *The Old Social Classes and the Revolutionary Movements of Iraq* (Princeton, NJ: Princeton University Press, 1978).

16. Ibid., for details on these actions.

17. The fact that this was a rally of Peace Partisans, a Soviet sponsored group, ties it to the Russians; also, according to Batatu, the leader of Iraq's Communist Party journeyed to Bulgaria just before the rally and subsequent riots erupted. I also should point out that a number of the Kurds who took part in the riots were followers of Mulla Mustafa Barzani, who at that time was closely allied with the Soviet Union. I have in my possession a photo of Mulla Mustafa in a Soviet general's uniform, given to me by an MI-6 officer later when I worked for intelligence.

18. Eagleton, *The Kurdish Republic of 1946.* In these early years, among the Communist Party's strongest adherents in Iraq were the Kurds, and this largely was due to Mulla Mustafa's connection to Moscow.

19. The best account of these twin events is Batatu's *The Old Social Class and the Revolutionary Movements of Iraq.* Batatu notes the sectarian character of both but also gives quite a strong argument for their class basis.

20. Which he did in 1961 by calling together the Iranians, Saudis, and Venzuelans for a meeting in Baghdad.

21. Qasem also made an ill fated attempt to invade and occupy Kuwait, the oil of which was then being exploited by the Americans and British.

22. One of Qasem's eccentricities, and he had a lot of these, was he lived in the Defense Ministry, sleeping on a camp bed.

23. See Uriel Dann, *Iraq Under Qassem* [sic] (London: Frederick A. Praeger, 1969).

24. Batatu, *The Old Social Classes and the Revolutionary Movements of Iraq*, 986.

25. Ibid.

26. The main reason the Communists rallying to Qasem lost out was he perversely refused to provide them with ammunition, and they were forced to fight with sticks and iron bars.

27. Michel Foucault, "Is It Useless to Revolt?" *Le Monde,* May 11–12, 1979. Foucault discusses this aspect of revolution in an article he wrote about the Iranian revolution under Khomeini. He describes revolution as "an uprooting that interrupts the unfolding of history." The uprooting, however it may have been triggered (in the case of Iraq by a coup), quickly develops into anarchy, and then, subsequently, those who presume to lead the revolt make efforts to contain the lawlessness. They justify their action on the basis that revolution ultimately is a progressive activity, meant to change society for the better; in other words, the society is urged to move on. Foucault notes, ironically, that "revolution (the conceptual notion) finds itself thus colonized by realpolitik." I believe that this is all very well for the professionals, to seek such a progression, but for the street people, the lawless elements, there is no incentive to move on. I think they know that, once the revolution settles down, that they will have to return to their routinized, and undoubtedly miserable, existences. So they try to perpetuate the violence, piling it on, till some power more ruthless than they can suppress them.

28. Batatu, *The Old Social Classes and the Revolutionary Movements in Iraq,* 1012.

29. Ibid., 1023.

30. Another significant difference: the Islamic Revolution was a part of the youth revolt that swept the world in the 1960s and through the 1970s, starting in Berkeley and spreading most spectacularly to Paris in 1968. This activity was largely fueled by television images; of course there was none of that with the Ba'th in 1963.

31. The Ba'th in its first appearance lasted 11 months.

32. Abdul Rahman offered a French firm, Enterprise de Rescherches et d' Activites Petrolieres (ERAP), a contract to develop an oil field which was part of the American-British consortium, IPC, nationalized by Qasem. To forestall this hand over (the theory goes), the Americans, through the CIA, engineered the removal of Abdul Rahman.

33. Batatu, *The Old Social Classes and the Revolutionary Movements in Iraq,* 1024.

34. The assassination was undertaken after a failed coup in Iraq.

35. Although Qasem began the nationalization in 1961, the process was not completed until 1975.

36. The oil cartel at this time controlled 70 percent of the world's known oil reserves. Thus, they could set world oil production and the price. Keeping oil

profitable meant keeping production down, and so they worked some fields and, in effect, shut in others. Iraq's fields were practically unexploited.

37. It is significant here that, under the Hashemites, who also had their police state, the police were the bailiwick of the Tikritis, of whom Hussein was one. So he had a ready-to-hand complement of tested police officers to draw on in building up the *Mukhabarat.*

38. Batatu, *The Old Social Classes and the Revolutionary Movements in Iraq,* 1095–96.

39. Said Aburish, *Saddam and the Politics of Revenge* (New York: Bloomsbury, 2000), 114.

40. Batatu, *The Old Social Classes and the Revolutionary Movements in Iraq.*

41. Also noteworthy is the fact that the British prior to their takeover of Iraq, under the mandate system, had hived off a portion of the southern province of Basrah, making what amounted to a British protectorate, Kuwait. It was in this way that Iraq practically lost its access to the Gulf.

42. I have talked to at least one intelligence officer (an Israeli, interestingly) who thought the Iraqis saved the Syrians' bacon, by turning up on the northern front as the Israelis were on the point of pushing the Syrians back to Damascus. The problem was the Syrians and Egyptians did not inform the Iraqis of their plan to go to war. As a consequence, the Ba'thists might have sat the war out. Instead they mobilized. Unfortunately, they had no tank transporters and so had to drive their tanks, on their treads, all the way to the front. Of course, there are many other experts who claim the Iraqi contribution was negligible.

43. That one exception (when they fought through the winter) was under the first Ba'th. The best treatment of Iraq's war against the Kurds, from a military standpoint, is Edgar O'Ballance's, *The Kurdish Struggle 1920–1994* (New York: St. Martin's Press, 1996.)

44. The reader should be aware that Hussein did not become Iraq's leader until 1979; until then he was Baker's right-hand man, and the real power behind the throne, so to speak.

45. The RCC was the real government of Iraq, a kind of junta. I will discuss more about it below. Here it is only necessary to know that it usually had no more than 8–10 members, all top Ba'thists. Under Hussein all these were civilians; only one army man served, Hussein's cousin Adnan Kharaillah.

46. Ninety-five percent of Iranians are Shias.

47. As part of this policy of fomenting revolt, the Iranians carried out assassination attempts against prominent Ba'thists. One against Tariq Aziz, the Iraqi vice president. And, of course, they also tried to assassinate Hussein. This was the Dujail affair, where Shias embedded in the village attempted to kill Hussein. He retaliated, executing a number of villagers he believed were complicit in the plot, and this was one of the alleged crimes for which he was tried after the war.

48. Of course, Khuzestan is also the site of the huge Iranian oil facility at Abadan. It is interesting that so many American leftists believe that Hussein went to war with Iran at the behest of the oil companies. The idea that the oil companies would like to have seen Iraq acquire Abadan is hard to figure.

49. I will discuss this episode in Chapter 4. It is of considerable significance, but very little has been made of it in the West, largely, I feel, because the principals—on the side of those opposing Iraq—do not come off looking well. The Barzani revolt had pretty much died down, and Hussein was in the process of negotiating a peace treaty, when Israel, the Shah of Iran, and Kissinger all intervened to talk Barzani into resuming the fight, which he did. When the Ba'thists nonetheless managed not just to survive but also appeared to be on the point of broadening the war to attack Iran, the conspirators pulled back, deserted the Kurds, and handed the Iraqis a victory of sorts. It was not a complete victory, since Iraq had to give up half the Shatt, which further constrained its access to the Gulf.

50. At least that is what he said; it is always possible he would have tried to hold on to Khuzestan. However, had he done that it would have seriously disturbed the balance of power in the Middle East, and along with the U.S. government, the Big Oil companies would have found this unacceptable, given that most of Iran's oil is located there.

51. Another innovation of the Guardsmen was they launched their attacks by night, which also significantly unnerved the Iraqis.

52. Since neither Iraq nor Iran permitted foreign observers at the front and neither gave out reliable information, losses in the war had to be guessed at. The American intelligence community generally figured that if a battle appeared to be a draw, the losses were three to one, in favor of the Iraqis (that was the population difference). Where the Iraqis clearly had won (which could be judged by the duration of the battle and by the fact that at the end the lines had not budged), the community noted this fact, ascribing a signifcant loss of troops (in this instance) to the Iranians.

53. The western intelligence services were not aware, or did not assign weight to, the Egyptians' advice for reforming the military intelligence arm. They inferred that the brothers fell out in a dispute over whom Hussein's daughter was to marry.

54. The timing of Reagan's move is interesting. It comes after the Iraqis held, and this says to me that the Americans were trying to balance the power equation. The Americans really wanted no winner in this war. I know many believe (and again, interestingly, these are mostly leftists in the United States who feel this way) that America colluded with Iraq, to go to war against Khomeini. In fact, to believe such is (in my view) naïve: the oil stakes were huge. Neither the U.S. government or the Big Oil companies wanted Iraq to acquire Khuzestan. Once the Iraqis were thrown back and in danger of losing the war, it then became safe for the United States to give it aid, to keep it fighting. Also, it is interesting that Reagan chose Solarz, a prominent U.S. Zionist, to be his emissary: most of the concessions Hussein was asked to make affected Israel.

55. Hussein agreed, among other things, to eject the May 15 organization, an anti-Israeli terrorist group, from Baghdad. He also agreed not to oppose Arafat, should the Palestinian attempt to enter into negotiations with the Israelis.

56. Up until 1982, Hussein was financing the war with his own money, but he ran through his gold reserves and became dependent not just on loans and grants from the sheikhs but loans from Europe as well.

57. American officers who toured the Iraqis' defenses outside Basrah claimed they were posh, with Coca Cola machines to dispense iced beverages and the like. Another wrinkle was that the troops could take French leave and go home, spend

awhile and then return, without punishment. However, the Ba'th conducted frequent sweeps through the capital and major cities; anyone found absent without leave was summarily shot. So the trick then was to get out and get back without incident.

58. It may even have been a concession to the Americans that the Iraqis would not pursue an aggressive strategy; that is, try to win. But that is pure speculation, I have no evidence for that.

59. The Islamists in Iran regarded the Shah's army as unreliable and thoroughly purged it on removing the Shah from power.

60. The cannon fodder (for such they were) were so-called *basij*. These were mostly rural recruits, without much sophistication. There are stories the Guards gave them silver keys which the Guardsmen told the *basij* were their keys to heaven, which they must present after death. The Guards would assign the *basij* to attack up to a certain point and stop. In that respect, one could say the Guards used the *basij* like human shells, firing them at a certain position, which, after impact, left them stranded; that is those that survived.

61. It is interesting that after SCIRI's propaganda effort failed, the Iranians desisted trying to subvert the Iraqis. Instead they swung over to carrying out sabotage against the Gulf sheikhs. Dawa was responsible for blowing up the American embassy in Kuwait in 1983.

62. Conversations with American officers who served in Iraq.

63. In Chapter 4 I discuss the contribution of the Iraqi Kurds in the war. Simply put, they fought on the side of Iraq, as paramilitaries, guarding the North against an Iranian breakthrough. As long as the Kurds stayed loyal (and they did throughout the war), the action in the North was limited, so sending the Popular Army there must have seemed a safe bet: they could not do any great damage.

64. See the U.S. Congressional investigation described in *The Tower Commission Report* (New York: Bantam Books, 1987).

65. They used it first at Haj Umran in the Kurdish area, and it was a fiasco. The Iraqis dropped the gas on peaks, where Revolutionary Guards units were dug in. The gas drifted into the valley, killing the Iraqi attackers.

66. Conversations with American officers stationed in Baghdad.

67. Recall that I said it was Solarz, an American Zionist, who was Reagan's emissary when the United States proposed backing Iraq in the war.

68. See *The Tower Commission Report*.

69. Not just of the U.S. embassy personnel in Tehran in 1979, but also in Lebanon, where Iranian surrogates of Hizbollah were seizing American hostages (in 1983–1984).

70. Essentially the Israelis were repeating their tactic of 1975, when they supplied American weapons to the Barzani Kurds, to benefit Iran against Iraq.

71. Technically, the weapons are not gratis, as they are supposed to be paid for. However, the way U.S. aid to Israel is dispensed, they never are.

72. However, the Israelis made up for their loss of revenue by getting promises from the Americans to replace the arms transferred to Iran.

73. The Contras then were fighting the Nicaraguan government, considered by the Americans to be a Soviet satellite.

74. All this came out in the Iran/Contra hearings in the U.S. Congress.

75. However, it had been abandoned in the war and was effectively a ghost town. This mitigated the loss somewhat.

76. See Stephen Pelletière, Douglas V. Johnson II, and Lief Rosenberger, *Iraqi Power and U.S. Security in the Middle East* (Carlisle, PA: Strategic Studies Institute, U.S. Army War College, 1990).

77. For Taylorizing the military see Enzo Traverso, *The Origins of Nazi Violence* (New York: The New Press, 2003), 78.

78. It was Rashid who made the famous crack about let the Iranians come, "we have the insecticide to kill these vermin." He was, of course, referring to gas, to break up the human wave attacks.

79. Details on this can be found in Stephen Pelletière, *The Iran-Iraq War: Chaos in a Vacuum* (Westport, CT: Praeger, 1992) and in a monograph I wrote with Douglas V. Johnson II, *Lesson Learned: The Iran-Iraq War* (Carlisle, PA: Strategic Studies Institute, U.S. Army War College, 1991).

80. I know this because I conducted the research. Pelletière, Johnson, and Rosenberger, *Iraqi Power and U.S. Security in the Middle East.*

81. See Pelletière, *The Iran-Iraq War: Chaos in a Vacuum.*

82. Ibid.

83. Ibid.

84. See Stephen Pelletière, *Iraq and the International Oil System* (Westport, CT: Praeger, 2001).

85. The transcript of Hussein's interview with Ambassador Glaspie appears in the *New York Times*, September 23, 1990.

86. The one exception to this collective view was the Defense Intelligence Agency's Middle East officer, Pat Lang. He alone counselled that not only would the Iraqis move against Kuwait but they also would succeed in the takeover before anyone could stop them.

87. At the tail end of the war, after Khomeini had admitted defeat, the Ba'thists sent troops into the North to establish a cordon sanitaire along the border with Iran, and they did it, as I say, to trap the Barzanis and also to cut off smuggling by the Kurds. They gave the Kurds living in the villages to be relocated the option of moving to new homes (which the Ba'thists provided for them) in the interior. Any Kurd who refused to move was killed. A war crime? Maybe. But certainly not genocide. This behavior replicates, I would say, the affair cited at the beginning of the chapter, where Baker Sidqi confronted the Assyrians who presumed to exit Iraq and return without permission of the Baghdad government. A government has the right to control commerce and movement across its borders. See the publication of the CIA, *Iraqs Weapons of Mass Destruction Programs* (Washington, DC: October 2002): 8 (http://www.fas.org/irp/cia/product/Iraq_Oct_2002.htm), where its says there is only one documented use of chemical weapons by Iraq for all of 1988, and in that instance there were relatively few casualties.

CHAPTER 3

1. I visited there three times: once as a journalist when I entered the country illegally from Iran (this was in the mid-1960s); once in the mid-1980s when I went

as an intelligence officer; and once in the early 1990s, before the first Iraq War, as a senior professor for the Strategic Studies Institute (SSI) at the U.S. Army War College in Carlisle, Pennsylvania.

2. As to where these ideas came from—some of them obviously derived from the British. The British and the Americans have a long-standing intelligence-sharing arrangement. Others date from the time of the Shah of Iran. Nixon deputized the Shah to become the Policeman of the Gulf, and for a time he exercised that role, along with collecting intelligence on Iraq which, SAVAK, the Iranian secret service, passed to the Americans. The Americans additionally may have gotten information from the oil companies, although I have no knowledge of that. And they definitely obtained information from the Israelis. The Israelis never had good contacts in Iraq, not after the Shah was overthrown—that did not stop them from trying to influence the Americans' policy on Baghad, as Iran/Contra shows.

3. "U.S. Plans to Reduce Forces in Iraq, with Help of Allies," *New York Times*, May 3, 2003.

4. For the British activity see Batatu, *The Old Social Classes and the Revolutionary Movements of Iraq;* for the Ottoman, Samira Haj, *The Making of Iraq, 1900–1963* (Albany: State University of New York Press, 1997).

5. Hussein came more and more to depend on a so-called *divan,* counselors he relied on, to the detriment of the RCC, and consequently to the party. Also, of course, he began grooming his sons to succeed him.

6. "Iraqi Tribes Asked to Help G.I.'s Say They Can't," *New York Times*, November 11, 2003.

7. Norberto Bobio in "Democracy and Invisible Government," *Telos* 52 (1982) cites the maxim that power is more effective the more [one] knows "he sees without being seen." The Mukhabarat was presumed to be everywhere. No one knew who was informing, hence it was politic to pay lip service to politically correct ideas.

8. In fact, the party began as a primarily Shia group. Its founder in Iraq (the party originally started in Syria by a Christian and a Sunni) was a Shia. See Batatu, *The Old Social Classes and the Revolutionary Movements in Iraq.*

9. The Twelver Shias, of which the Iraqis and Iranians are part, believe that the 12th Imam is occluded, and that he will return to rule the faithful. Until he comes, all temporal authority is rejected. This is what drove the late Shah to open enmity with the Shia clerics, whom he called black communists.

10. See Yitzhak Nakash, *The Shias of Iraq* (Princeton, NJ: Princeton University Press, 1994), 4.

11. See Batatu, *The Old Social Class and the Revolutionary Movements of Iraq.*

12. This ultimatum also was precipitated by an attempted coup against the Ba'th, in which the Shah was implicated. This took place in 1970.

13. Something like this occurred in Egypt where Nasser delivered a similar ultimatum to the Italian community, extensive in both Cairo and Alexandria. There, too, as in Iraq, many Italians left Egypt for Italy rather than accept Nasser's conditions.

14. The Iranian influence also obtained but to a lesser degree in the North. When I, as a reporter, went into Iraq in the sixties to cover the Barzani revolt, the Shah's secret service smuggled me in and met me when I came out. The service (SAVAK) was constantly intriguing with the Barzanis.

15. See Richard Augustus Norton, *Amal and the Shia: Struggle for the Soul of Lebanon* (Austin: University of Texas Press, 1987). The Shah practiced a similar kind of subversion through the Shia clergy in Lebanon.

16. "Iraqi Intermarriages Defy Civil War Spectre," *Aljazeera*, March 23, 2006.

17. I once asked a high-ranking, and very knowledgeable, American intelligence officer this question, and he answered, "Well, they're sheep." I thought, well, if they are sheep, they fight like tigers. This was 1982, just after the largely Shia Iraqi army had stopped the Iranians' invasion of Basrah, inflicting a huge toll in Iranian lives.

18. From conversations with U.S. officers stationed in Baghdad.

19. See Pelletière, *The Iran-Iraq War: Chaos in a Vacuum.*

20. Another belief of the Americans was that Hussein ruled as an autocrat. In the RCC, all decisions were taken by consensus, which led to marathon sessions while the members argued matters out. This practice eroded over the years, but during the war it remained.

21. In 1973, there was another coup against the Ba'th initiated by the then-interior minister, and he was a Shia.

22. It is interesting that when Iraq invaded Iran in 1980, Hussein was informed by Iranian expatriates—former officials of the Shah—that the Iranians would welcome the Iraqis with open arms. One could say that hyping conditions is an expatriate flaw.

23. The pilgrimage is held during the Shia observance of Ashura, but also devout Shias want to be buried in Najaf and so seek to bring the deceased to Iraq no matter where they live.

24. When the Americans failed to close the border immediately after taking over in Iraq, all sorts of Iranian subversives flooded across under the cover of the pilgrimage (as I will discuss in the next chapter). Similarly, when the Americans held elections in 2005, Iran sent Iranians over to vote, thus rigging the election.

25. As an intelligence officer I would make frequent trips to the Middle East. I always could gauge the amount of religious feeling wherever I visited simply by noting the profusion of beards on the men and veils on the women. This was a marked phenomenon in Egypt, for example, when Gadhafi strove to make his influence felt there.

26. See Pelletière, *The Iran-Iraq War: Chaos in a Vacuum.*

27. Khomeini despised the secular Ba'thists, as much as any Iranian cleric, and after Hussein expelled him this only increased his antipathy to the Iraqi regime. In addition to trying to export the Islamic Revolution to Iraq for reasons of wanting to promote Shia Islam among its millions of co-religionists, one also could say he promoted rebellion as part of a personal grudge.

28. Pelletière, *The Iran-Iraq War: Chaos in a Vacuum.*

29. Nakash, *The Shias of Iraq.*

30. In this respect, Hussein can be compared to Mustafa Kemal Ataturk of Turkey. In fact, there are many parallels one could draw between the two leaders.

31. There was another good reason for upgrading women: during the Iran-Iraq War, with Iraq under extraordinary mobilization, most men were at the front; women were essential to run the bureaucracy. But note, the women would have been

of no use in this regard, if the Ba'thists had not instituted a policy of insisting they be educated, up to the university level, and that was a policy in place before the war.

32. Both Barzani's Kurdish Democratic Party and Jelal Talabani's Patriotic Union of Kurdistan have over the years functioned as anti-Kurdish nationalism forces. The KDP allowed itself to be used by Khomeini to crush the Iranian Kurdish Democratic Party (IKDP), and both the KDP and PUK teamed up with the Turks in the 1990s to drive the Turkish Kurdish nationalist guerrillas of the Kurdish Workers Party (PKK) out of northern Iraq which they were using as a safe haven.

33. See Stephen Pelletière, *The Kurds: An Unstable Element in the Persian Gulf* (Boulder, CO: Westview Press, 1998.)

34. Something he did in the 1970s.

35. In 1964, when I went out, I asked Barzani why, after Aref came to power in 1963, the old chief agreed to a truce with no conditions, when one would have expected him to bargain for rights. He said the American ambassador had advised him to. Given that Aref, of all the republican rulers, came closest to allying with the West, this seems to throw light on how Barzani operated.

36. The arrangement was that the Kurds were organized into paramilitary formations, called the *fursan*. These units were solely to guard the North against Iranian invasion tries; they could not be ordered to serve anywhere outside the North.

37. See David Stevenson, *Cataclysm: The First World War as Political Tragedy* (New York: Basic Books, 2004), 151, for a discussion of casualties from gassing in World War I. Stevenson cites a casualty figure of perhaps half a million on the western front, but only 25,000 fatalities. This was over the course of the whole war, and the combatants used 124,208 tons of chemicals in the war. Also see John Mueller, *Overblown* (New York: Free Press, 2006), 18, on the lethality of chemicals. "Although gas was used extensively in World War I, it accounted for less than 1 percent of the battle deaths. It took over one ton of gas to produce a single fatality." The problem with gas is it is extremely volatile. It can be dissipated by wind currents; it tends to settle into declivities in the ground, and it is useless in wet weather. The notorious instance of the Nazis using it against concentration camp inmates illustrates the point I am trying to make. The number of victims was large because the gas was released in a closed room; the victims could not escape. I was told by a U.S. chemical weapons expert for the army that, in order to kill hundreds of thousands of Kurds with gas (as the gassing proponents allege), the Ba'thists would have had to enclose the whole of northern Iraq under a bell jar and pump the gas in. The reader might also want to consult my op-ed piece, "A War Crime or an Act of War?" *New York Times,* January 31, 2001, where I discuss the infamous Halabja incident.

38. There are many related arguments I could bring to bear to throw doubt on the legitimacy of the claims about the Anfal. However, this one, about the logistics of the affair, I think is clinching. To be sure, the casualty figure (of the Kurds supposedly gassed) keeps going up and down. I have seen figures as low as 30,000 and even above 200,000. Given the circumstances under which gas would have had to be employed against the Kurds (the Anfal is only supposed to have lasted six months!), all of these figures—even the lowest—are incredible.

39. In the 1980s such scholarship on Iraq as was available in English was outdated, heavily influenced by work done by British scholars in the colonial period.

Hannah Batatu's magistral tome, *The Old Social Classes and the Revolutionary Movements in Iraq,* did not appear until 1982, and then, it was my experience, many analysts were unacquainted with it. Also, in the 1990s many anti-Saddam, anti-Ba'th books circulated. These were worthless. For example, Kanan Makiya's book (cited above) *Republic of Fear,* and Judith Miller and Laurie Mylroie, *Saddam Hussein and the Crisis in the Gulf* (New York: New York Times Books, 1990). Unfortunately, these latter were avidly consumed by the neo-cons. Wolfowitz was a big fan of Mylroie.

40. Rupert Smith, *The Art of War: The Utility of Force in the Modern World* (New York: Penguin Press, 2005). Smith says something interesting about that first Iraq War and the Iraqis' performance in it. He says that Hussein deliberately allowed the Americans to build up their force, knowing that once America called his bluff he could not win against them, but he was conscious that he must not be seen to be humiliated. By allowing the Americans to assemble a great host to pose against him, he (Hussein) was then enabled to withdraw from Kuwait without losing face, since by that time the odds against him could be perceived as overwhelming. Clearly, if Smith is right, Hussein was playing to the gallery: he had at all costs to maintain the respect of his fellow Arabs (and his own people), even at the cost of losing a few divisions of his troops, which were caught in Kuwait.

41. "Jobs at Risk, Ex-Iraqi Soldiers Vow Fight if Allies Don't Pay," *New York Times,* May 25, 2003. What needs to be borne in mind, too, is that Iraq at the time of the occupation was awash with weapons. Not just the army men, but all male Iraqis were armed.

42. "Violence in Iraq Spreads; Six British Soldiers Are Killed," *New York Times,* June 25, 2003.

43. "U.S. Commander in Iraq Says Yearlong Tours Are Option to Combat 'Guerrilla War,'" *New York Times,* July 17, 2003.

44. "3 G.I.'s Killed in Iraq Capital, One at Campus," *New York Times,* July 7, 2003.

45. "G.I. Dies, Others Are Wounded in New Ambushes in Iraq," *New York Times,* June 28, 2003.

46. "G.I.'s in Iraqi City Are Stalked by Faceless Enemies at Night," *New York Times,* June 11, 2003.

47. "G.I.'s on the Road from Kuwait to Baghdad Still Run a Gauntlet of Danger," *New York Times,* March 9, 2004.

48. "Iraqi Saboteurs Goal: Disrupt the Occupation," *New York Times,* June 28, 2003.

49. "A Rash of Pipeline Fires Is Keeping Workers Busy," *New York Times,* June 24, 2003.

50. "Iraqi Saboteurs Goal: Disrupt the Occupation." Another instance was the destruction of a whole warehouse of spare parts for Iraq's electrical grid. With the Americans scrambling to get the utilities back in operation, this was a serious blow.

51. "Iraqi Insurgents Take a Page from Afghan 'Freedom Fighters,'" *New York Times,* November 9, 2003.

52. "Latest Bombing Strikes at Iraqis Working with the U.S.," *New York Times,* July 6, 2003.

53. "Iraqi Rebels Refine Bomb Skills, Pushing G.I. Toll Ever Higher," *New York Times,* June 22, 2005.

54. Ibid.

55. "11 Die in Baghdad as Car Bomb Hits Jordan Embassy," *New York Times,* August 8, 2003.

56. "Huge Suicide Blast Demolishes U.N. Headquarters in Baghdad; Top Officials Among 17 Dead," *New York Times,* August 20, 2003.

57. "Car Bomb In Iraq Kills 95," *New York Times,* August 30, 2003.

58. "Car Bomb Kills 6 at Baghdad Hotel; at Least 35 Hurt," *New York Times,* October 13, 2003.

59. "Wolfowitz's Hotel Is Attacked in Baghdad," *New York Times,* August 26, 2003.

60. "At Least 26 Killed in a Bombing of Italian Compound In Iraq," *New York Times,* November 13, 2003.

61. "Commander Doesn't Expect More Foreign Troops in Iraq," *New York Times,* September 26, 2003.

62. "Terror Group Seen as Back Inside Iraq," *New York Times,* August 10, 2003.

63. Stephen Pelletière, *The Kurds and Their Agas* (Carlisle, PA: The Strategic Studies Institute, U.S. Army War College, 1991).

64. It may have been that these were the Fayali Kurds, Shias, who left Iraq in response to the 1970s ultimatum of Hussein. If so, they later turn up providing the base for Talabani's PUK.

65. The original evidence was "discovered" in January 2004. See "Up to 16 Die in Gun Battles in Sunni Areas of Iraq," *New York Times,* January 27, 2004. The report that it was faked appeared in "Military Plays Up Role of Zarkawi," *Washington Post,* April 10, 2006.

66. "U.S. Officers in Iraq Find Few Signs of Infiltration by Foreign Fighters," *New York Times,* November 19, 2003.

67. In 1990, in discussions I held at the U.S. Embassy in Amman, Jordan, I was told this. At the time, the proficiency and strength of these smugglers' clans was well known. I was told they were using the latest up-to-date equipment to run the border, including armed personnel carriers.

68. This can be illustrated by consulting a map of where the clashes occurred: they came all along the river route leading from the border to the interior. Smugglers to move over a huge desert expanse must keep close to the available water supplies.

69. "Up to 16 Die in Gun Battles in Sunni Areas of Iraq."

70. "Iraqi Nationalism Takes Root, Sort Of," *New York Times,* April 25, 2003.

71. Ibid.

72. "7 U.S. Soldiers Die in Iraq as a Shite Militia Rises Up," *New York Times,* April 5, 2003.

73. Batatu, *The Old Social Classes and the Revolutionary Movements in Iraq,* 134.

74. "Account of Broad Shiite Revolt Contradicts White House Stand," *New York Times,* April 8, 2004.

75. "Mob Violence in Iraq," *New York Times,* August 6, 2003.

76. "U.S. May Delay Departure of Some Troops in Iraq," *New York Times,* April 8, 2003.

77. "U.S. Forces Rush to Send Tanks to Iraq," *New York Times,* April 29, 2003.

78. "Military Mulls Boosting Iraq Force," *Chicago Tribune,* April 7, 2003.

79. "Look at U.S. Military Deaths in Iraq," *Associated Press,* April 14, 2003.

80. "Ex-Rivals Uniting," *New York Times,* April 18, 2004.

CHAPTER 4

1. "Pentagon Sending a Team of Exiles to Help Run Iraq," *New York Times,* April 26, 2003.

2. "Iraqi Exiles, Backed by U.S., Return to Invent a Country," *New York Times,* May 4, 2003.

3. "Pentagon Sending a Team of Exiles to Help Run Iraq."

4. For background on Chalabi see "Chalabi, as Iraqi Deputy, Gets a Cautious Welcome in Washington," *New York Times,* November 9, 2003.

5. For example, Chalabi was wanted in Jordan on an embezzling charge.

6. "Granting Power to Baathists a Concern for Iraqi Leader," *New York Times,* May 1, 2003.

7. "Iraqi Leaders Gather Under U.S. Tent," *Washington Post,* April 16, 2003.

8. "Mob Kills 2 Clerics at Shiite Shrine," *Washington Post,* April 11, 2003.

9. David Ignatius, "Regime Change's Regional Ripples," *Washington Post,* April 15, 2003. Ignatius reports that it might have been Dawa that did the deed. But, as Ignatius may not have been aware, Dawa and SCIRI are practically one and the same; both are Iranian surrogates, and originally SCIRI incorporated Dawa.

10. "Iraqis More Bemused Than Enthused by Cleric," *New York Times,* May 12, 2003.

11. Indeed in some areas—the mountainous Kurdish region, for example—it is impossible to police.

12. "Gingerly, Pro-Iranian Iraqi Muslim Group Lobbies for Washington's Favor," *New York Times,* May 7, 2003.

13. See Nicholas Kristof, "Diplomacy at Its Worst," *New York Times,* April 23, 2007. Since I wrote, this evidence has come out indicating United States-Iran talks on possible cooperation over the occupation of Iraq were going on right up to the actual invasion. So, maybe the SCIRI people were involved.

14. "Gingerly, Pro-Iranian Iraqi Muslim Group Lobbies for Washington's Favor."

15. "Iran Said to Send Agents into Iraq," *New York Times,* April 23, 2003.

16. This was not a negligible force: the brigadistas may have numbered as high as 10,000.

17. "Militia Trained in Iran Controls a Tense Town," *New York Times,* June 27, 2003.

18. "Gingerly, Pro-Iranian Iraqi Muslim Group Lobbies for Washington Favor."

19. Chalabi, over the years, had ingratiated himself with the Israelis, and of course most of the neo-cons were pro-Israel—moreover, they were Likudniks (more on that below).

20. "Granting Power to Baathists a Concern for Iraqi Leader," *New York Times,* May 1, 2003.

21. Actually Talabani went over to the side of the Ba'thists more than once. He also did it in the sixties.

22. See "Kurds Destroy Shrine in Rage at Leadership," *New York Times,* March 17, 2006, for Kurdish opposition to Talabani and Barzani.

23. From conversations with officers who were there.

24. "Leading Iraqi Shiite Cleric Emerges to Meet U.S. Ally," *New York Times,* June 6, 2003.

25. Sistani had been mentored by the father of the murdered Khoi.

26. "U.S. Set to Name Civilian to Oversee Iraq," *New York Times,* May 2, 2003.

27. "Government Planning Meeting Is Denounced as Unrepresentative by Uninvited," *Washington Post,* April 16, 2003.

28. "In Reversal, Plan for Iraq Self-Rule Has Been Put Off," *New York Times,* May 12, 2003.

29. Ibid.

30. "Shiite Group Says U.S. Is Reneging on Interim Rule, *New York Times,* May 19, 2003.

31. Ibid.

32. "Cleric Calls for Pluralistic Government in Iraq," *New York Times,* May 25, 2003.

33. Support for this theory comes from a *New York Times* dispatch which reveals that the news of Sistani's disagreeing with Bremer came from a spokesman for SCIRI, not from the ayatollah himself. "Leading Iraqi Shiite Cleric Emerges to Meet U.S. Ally," *New York Times,* June 6, 2003.

34. Ibid.

35. Actually some of them, as with the two Kurdish leaders, were already in Iraq, set up in the free zone in the North.

36. It may have been the case that the Communists got on the list because Indyk needed representatives of the secular opposition—that is, a group with long-standing involvement in Iraq. (Allawi and Chalabi formed their parties comparatively recently.) There was not any such group except the Communists, a party which Hussein decimated in the late 1970s, driving all of its leaders into exile in Europe (the ones he did not execute). It also may have been the case that the Kurdish leaders spoke up for the Communists' inclusion, as the Communist Party in Iraq lived for years under the protection of Barzani, and became practically a client of the Kurds.

37. "In Reversal, Plan for Iraqi Self-Rule Has Been Put Off," *New York Times,* May 17, 2003.

38. "As Iraqis' Dissatisfaction Grows, U.S. Offers Them a Greater Political Role," *New York Times,* June 7, 2003.

39. It is possible to speculate that the U.S. military may have become involved. The U.S. Central Command (CENTCOM) had a long-standing dislike for

Chalabi, for one, and although the Army attempted to work with his organization in the lead up to the war, immediately after the victory was declared problems developed. In several instances actual clashes took place between militiamen associated with Chalabi and the U.S. Army, and the military also shut down several of his offices. Along with that, the two Kurdish leaders, Jelal Talabani and Masoud Barzani, would not work with each other. It is possible that, with violence spiraling out of control in Iraq, the military signaled Washington a new approach was needed, and that is when Garner was removed and Bremer sent out.

40. The Barzanis have a long history of cultivating the American Jewish community. Mulla Mustafa, the old chief, at one point went so far as to say, if he could create an independent state in the North of Iraq, he would turn the Kurds' oil over to Israel.

41. For background on this, see Thomas Ricks, *Fiasco: The American Military Adventure in Iraq* (New York: Penguin Press, 2006).

42. Chalabi, at one point, was actually exposed (by the FBI) as trading classified secrets with the Iranians. But he is so well in with the neo-cons, and with the American Jewish community, the scandal, if it has not been hushed up, has been allowed to languish. Chalabi continues to cut a figure in Washington, he frequently addresses the American Enterprise Institute, and so on.

43. In other words, turn it back to the way it was under the Shah, when the Iranian consul-general in Basrah ran the South.

44. I do not think that the neo-cons seriously believed they could take over Iraq until 9/11 happened. Then they viewed this as a deus ex machina: they could tie Iraq into that horror and promote the takeover on the basis Hussein and Osama bin Laden were allies.

45. The reader must keep in mind that, from 1991 on, the warlords practically controlled the North.

46. One needs to be aware that the two enclaves claimed by the warlords are inconveniently located: they constitute virtual islands surrounded by potential enemies. The two were constantly seeking to maintain friendly borders at their backs. Talabani, in particular, is vulnerable in this way. It would make sense for him, while keeping up a pretense of cooperating with the Americans, to hedge his bets by keeping lines open to Tehran.

47. "Cleric Wants Iraqis to Write Constitution," *New York Times,* July 1, 2003.

48. "Iraqis Will Join Governing Council U.S. Is Setting Up," *New York Times,* July 8, 2003.

49. "Iraqi Factions Agree on Members of Governing Council," *New York Times,* July 13, 2003.

50. Kurds Are Flocking to Kirkuk, Laying Claim to Land and Oil," *New York Times,* December 29, 2005.

51. "Erdogan: Iraq's Division Would Spell Disaster," *Turkish Daily News,* November 29, 2006.

52. "Council Picks a Cabinet to Run Key State Affairs," *New York Times,* September 2, 2003.

53. "Powell Gives Iraq Six Months to Write New Constitution," *New York Times,* September 26, 2003.

54. "U.S. Is to Return Power to Iraqis as Early as June," *New York Times,* November 15, 2003.

55. "Police Seize Forged Ballots Headed to Iraq from Iran," *New York Times,* December 14, 2005.

56. "U.S., Britain Holding 10,000 Prisoners in Iraq," *Agence France Presse,* December 28, 2004, http://www.truthout.org/cgi-bin/artman/exec/view.cgi/42/8061.

57. "Iraqi Officials to Allow Vote by Expatriates," *New York Times,* November 5, 2004.

58. Peter Graff, "Iraq Signs Military Pact with Iran," *Reuters,* July 7, 2005, http://www.truthout.org/cgi-bin/artman/exec/view.cgi/37/12462.

59. "Saddam's Cousin Acknowledges Giving Orders," *Associated Press,* January 28, 2007.

60. It might even have been Iran. The mullahs had to fear the formation of a native Iraqi Shia/Sunni coalition, and there were signs of just such a development materializing. By blowing up the mosque and pinning it on Sunnis, Iran could hope to prevent this from happening, since the Shias could then be expected to turn on their erstwhile Sunni allies.

61. "Failing to Disband Militias, U.S. Moves to Accept Them," *New York Times,* May 25, 2004.

62. "Shias, Sunnis Form Ghettos," *Aljazeera,* July 29, 2006.

63. Graff, "Iraq Signs Military Pact with Iran."

64. Ibid.

65. Talabani was at that time the principal ideologue of the Kurdish nationalist movement in Iraq. He was also a leader of the Kurdish Democratic Party, which as I said in the last chapter was presided over by Mulla Mustafa Barzani. He and Barzani had had a falling out and the old chief drove the younger man into exile in Tehran, where Talabani claimed the protection of the Shah.

66. "Kurds Are Illegally Jailing Arabs and Others, U.S. Says," *New York Times,* June 16, 2005.

67. The Turkomans are ethnic Turks, domociled in and citizens of Iraq. They predominantly reside in the Kurdish area and have long been alienated from the majority Kurdish community.

68. "Annan: Iraq was Safer under Saddam," *Guardian Unlimited,* December 4, 2006, http://www.guardian.co.uk/international/story/0,,1963611,00.html.

69. "Civilian Death Toll Reaches New High in Iraq, U.N. Says," *New York Times,* November 23, 2006.

70. "Rice Backs 'Worthwhile' Iraq War," *BBC News,* December 22, 2006, http://newsvote.bbc.co.uk/mpapps/pagetools/print/news.bbc.co.uk/2/hi/middle_east/6202469.stm.

71. "Iraq a 'Work of Art in Progress' Says U.S. General After 49 Die," *Guardian of London,* November 3, 2006.

72. "U.S. Considers Private Iraqi Force to Guard Sites," *New York Times,* July 18, 2003.

73. "Iraqi Political Parties Will Form Militia to Work with American Forces," *New York Times,* December 4, 2003.

74. Joseph Biden and Leslie Gelb, "Unity Through Autonomy in Iraq," *New York Times,* May 1, 2006.

CONCLUSION

1. The K Street Project was an attempt by Republicans to coerce the Washington lobbying establishment into deserting the Democrats by insisting the lobbies hire Republican interns off the Hill. Had this scheme not been frustrated, which I assume it now has (thanks to the 2006 elections), the lobbies would in effect have become an arm of the Republican Party.

2. With the collapse of the Soviet Union, there developed a move in Congress to shift money formerly allotted to the Defense Department to domestic spending. Hence, in the military's view, the late 1980s was the period of the great Train Wreck.

3. Stephen Pelletière, *America's Oil Wars* (Westport, CT: Praeger, 2004).

4. A task that was facilitated by Indyk's purging of the Arabists in the government under Clinton.

5. "The War Dividend: The British Companies Making a Fortune out of Conflict-Riven Iraq," *The Independent,* http://news.independent.co.uk/world/middle_east/article350959.ece.

6. "Document Says Oil Chiefs Met with Cheney Task Force," *Washington Post,* November 16, 2005; "U.S. Wants New Iraq Oil Law So Foreign Firms Can Take Part," *Agence France Presse,* July 18, 2006; "Exxon Reports $10.49 Billion Profit in Quarter," *New York Times,* October 26, 2006; "Iraq Official Calls for Oil Partnerships," *Associated Press,* September 11, 2006.

7. "Iraq War Good For Israel: Olmert," *Reuters,* November 10. 2006.

8. "Bush, Fund-Raiser in Chief, Hits the Trail in Earnest," *New York Times,* October 3, 2006.

9. "Ties to GOP Trumped Know-How Among Staff Sent to Iraq," *Washington Post,* September 17, 2006.

10. See Pelletière, *Iraq and the International Oil System* and *America's Oil Wars.*

11. "Saudis Halt Eurofighter Talks in Bid to End Graft Inquiry," *Financial Times,* November 28, 2006.

12. "Inquiry Opened into Israeli Use of U.S. Bombs," *New York Times,* August 25, 2006.

13. "Attacks Qualify as War Crimes, Officials Say," *New York Times,* July 20, 2006.

14. "Lancet Author Answers Your Questions," *BBC News,* October 30, 2006.

15. Recall neo-con David Wurmser's scheme to restore the Hashemites.

Index

constitution, writing, 86, 94, 95
Constitution Party, 34
contract with American, 105

Dawa Party, 45, 85, 89, 94, 126 n.61,
    133 n.9
"Death squads," 10, 11
defense contractors. *See* arms industry
Defense Intelligence Agency (DIA), 66
De Gaury, Gerald, 27–28, 29
Divan, 128 n.5
Doctrine of overwhelming force, 8
Dresden, Germany, 17
Druze community of Lebanon, 48
Dujail affair, 124 n.47

East Germany, 37
education reforms under Ba'th, 39
Egypt: 1973 Arab–Israeli War, 40;
    alliance with Iraq following 1963
    coup, 34–35; Aref rebuffed by, 35;
    critique of Iraqi army, 43;
    demonstrations against the war, 19;
    failed attempt at alliance with Syria,
    35; Italian community within, 128
    n.13; lack of support for Ba'thists,
    22–23; proposed alliance with Iraq
    under Nasser, 30; religious level
    within, 129 n.25; revolt by Nasser,
    30; support for U.S. War on
    terrorism, 109–10
elderly as resistance fighters, 13–14
elections, 80, 86, 94–98, 100, 129
    n.24. *See also* interim authority
electric grids, 18, 25, 68
Enterprise de Rescherches et d'
    Activites Petrolieres (ERAP), 123
    n.32
Erdogan, Recip Tayyip, 6
Euphrates, 9, 10, 12–13, 20, 71
European opposition to war, 17
expatriates of Iran, 129 n.22
expatriates of Iraq, 2–3, 78–103; as
    agents of Iran, 77, 88, 89, 90, 97; al
    Sadr as rival to, 73; Clinton
    administration support for, 80–81,
    84–85; constitution to be written by,
    94, 95; cooperation with Bremer,

73; core of government council
    formed by, 2–3, 92; desire to create
    separate Kurdish state, 89, 94;
    illegitimacy of new government
    formed by, 100; institutionalization
    of role, 92, 97; on interim authority
    formed under Bremer, 85–88, 91;
    Iraqi perception of, 82, 85; militias
    of, 82, 89, 102; return to Iraq
    following second Iraq War, 85; role
    in Iran–Iraq War, 2–3; role in
    planning invasion, 80; on
    sectarianism, 60; U.S. goals opposed
    by, 89; on WMD, 66. *See also
    individuals by name*

Faisal, Prince of Saudi Arabia, 22–23
Faisal I of Iraq, 27–28
al Fakhri, Hisham, 46–47, 50, 51
Fallujah, 29, 71–72, 75, 95–96
"Fanatics," U.S. and British perception
    of, 9–12. *See also* resistance
Farouk I of Egypt, 30
Fayali Kurds, 132 n.64
Fedayeen, 12, 13–15, 117 n.31, 119
    n.69
Feith, Douglas, 66, 87, 107
Fifth Column of Iran, 45, 60, 74–75
51st Regular Army Division, 9–10
first Iraq War: carpet bombing, 4;
    conventional fighting of, 14; Iraqi
    infrastructure damaged during, 4;
    Kurdish nationalism, 62; no-fly zone
    over northern Iraq set by U.S., 81–
    82; power consolidated by Ba'thists
    following, 84; sanctions following,
    4, 84; Turkish support for U.S. dur-
    ing, 115–16 n.2; U.S. ground troops
    committed during, 106
The Follow Up Committee of Iraq, 37
food shortages. *See* humanitarian
    crises
Foucault, Michel, 123 n.27
France, 28, 123 n.30
Franks, Tommy, 7–8, 10, 11, 17, 57
free officers, 122 n.13
fundamentalism, 110
Fursan, 130 n.36

Gadhafi, Muammar, 129 n.25
Garner, Jay, 82–83, 85, 87, 88, 91
gas attacks. *See* chemical attacks
genocidal campaigns vs. Kurds, 27, 28, 51, 55, 65
Germany, 28–29. *See also* East Germany; Nazis
Glaspie, April, 54
Golden Mosque in Samara, 99
Gordon, Michael, 17, 116 n.7, 117 n.22
Governing council, 4, 92–97. *See also* occupation phase
Government ministries, attacks on, 68
Great Britain. *See* Britain
Guerilla warfare, 14–16, 67–71, 111. *See also* resistance

Habaniyah, Iraq, 28
Haj Umran, 126 n.65
al-Hakim, Abdul Aziz, 45, 61, 96, 97
al-Hakim, Muhammad Bakr: as agent of Iran, 79–80, 89, 90; alleged murder of Khoi by, 79, 90; death of, 69, 97–98; departure from Iraq, 45, 61, 82; desire to lead Iraqi Shia community, 73; on elections, 80; on interim authority, 83–84, 85–87; return to Iraq following second Iraq War, 85, 90; SCIRI directed by, 45; U.S. treatment of during exile, 80–81
Hashemites of Iraq, 29, 39, 72, 81, 93
Hashemites of Jordan, 39
HCD (high collateral damage) bombs, 17, 18–19, 21–22. *See also* air war (U.S.)
Herold, Marc, 20
Hizbollah, 49, 110, 126 n.69. *See also* Lebanon
holy sites: oil wealth at, 109; resisters within, 19, 20
humanitarian crises, 18, 20, 21. *See also* genocidal campaigns vs. Kurds
human wave attacks, 42–43, 45, 46, 52, 53, 112
Hussein, Barzan, 43, 98
Hussein, Sabawi, 43
Hussein, Saddam: advisors to, 128 n.5;

on Arab–Israeli conflict, 39; on Arab unifications plans, 39–40; Assad vs., 70–71; as Baker's right-hand man, 36–37, 124 n.44; Ba'th converted into mass movement by, 37–38, 39, 58–59, 62; centralized regime of, 57–58; distrust between army and, 40–41; Dujail affair, 124 n.47; early history with the Ba'th, 36–40; education of, 34; expatriates ridiculed by, 85; imported goods to Iraq encouraged by, 39; Iran–Iraq War under, 3, 42, 44, 50–52, 54, 55, 66; Iraqi Shias vs., 59–60, 61; on Israel, 47–48; Kurdish loyalty bought by, 65; location of prior to invasion of Iraq, 7, 21; Mukhabarat (secret police) under, 37, 38; old line Ba'thists removed by, 39; promoted as ally to Bin Laden, 135 n.44; recruitment for Republican Guard by, 51–52; Sadr executed by, 61; Soviets and, 121 n.1; statues of, 23; as Tikriti, 59, 124 n.37; trial and execution of, 98, 124 n.47; tribal authority undermined by, 57–58; U.S. expectations of during second Iraqi War, 9–10, 22, 91; withdrawal of Popular Army from frontlines by, 46
Hussein, Uday, 12
Hussein, Watban, 43

IED's (improvised explosive devices), 69, 110–11
Ignatius, David, 133 n.9
imported goods to Iraq, 39
INA (Iraqi National Accord), 76, 89
INC, 89
India, 30
Indyk, Martin, 80, 84–85
informants within Iraq, 38, 40–41, 42, 93
insurgents. *See* resistance
interim authority, 83–92. *See also* elections
interior ministry, 97–100, 129 n.21
invasion phase, 6–25; air war vs. Baghdad, 16, 24; casualties during,

leaders, 59, 61; implicated in attempted coup vs. Ba'th, 128 n.12; Nixon and, 128 n.2; overthrow of, 34, 112. *See also* Iran

Shamir, Itzak, 47–48, 49. *See also* Israel

Sharon, Ariel, 48

Shatt al Arab, 41, 52, 64

Shia community: areas of control allotted to, 74; army units during second Iraq War, 66; benefited by Ba'thists, 38–39; British perception of, 10; clerics' distance from politics, 79; fetwa issued by Sistani, 23–24, 92; Golden Mosque in Samara, 99; governing council, representation within, 92, 93–94; informants of Ba'thists watching, 41, 42; of Iran, 62; during Iran–Iraq War, 41, 60, 61; Iraqi army composed of, 14, 44, 45, 60; Khomeini's attempts to spread revolution to, 45, 61; within Lebanon, 48; majority constituted by, 96; national sentiment of, 43; patron saint of, 20; pilgrimages of, 60–61; policy dictated by Najaf School, 84; within RCC, 60; resistance by, 73–74; Sunnis and, 39–40, 60, 61–62; United Shia Alliance, 96, 97; U.S. perception of, 9–10, 18, 45, 58–62, 65–66, 74, 81; Wahhabis vs., 70

Shrines. *See* holy sites

Shurugis, 72

Sidqi, Bakr, 27–28, 127 n.87

Sistani, Ayatollah Ali: alliance with Barzani, 90, 92; alliance with Hakim, 89, 90; anointed as spiritual guide by U.S., 76, 82; on elections, 96; fetwa issued by, 23–24, 92; on interim authority, 83–84, 85–87, 90, 92; refusal to condemn Sadr, 76

Smith, Rupert, 131 n.40

smuggling by Kurds, 63–64, 71, 75, 127 n.87

social security, 108

Solarz, Stephen, 43, 47

South Yemen, 40

Soviet Union: Barzani alliance, 122 nn.17, 18, collapse of, 105, 106, 109; Iraq as former satellite of, 26, 30–31, 32, 37–38, 121 n.1

Staatssicherheit (Stasi), 37, 38, 50, 93

starvation. *See* humanitarian crises

Stevenson, David, 130 n.37

students. *See* youth movements

suicide bombers, 13, 15, 19, 69–70, 111. *See also* resistance

Sulaymaniyah, Iraq, 82

Sunni community: boycott of elections, 96; converts to Shias, 61–62; formation of enclaves during occupation, 99; intermarriage with Shias, 60; representation on governing council, 92, 93–94; U.S. perception of, 10, 58–59

Supreme Council of the Islamic Revolution in Iraq (SCIRI). *See* SCIRI

Susangard battle, 42

Syria, 28, 35, 39, 40, 70–71

Talabani, Jelal: AIPAC connections, 87; career of, 100–101; as elected official, 97, 100–101; on interim authority, 85–87; Iranian alliance, 90; PUK of, 89, 130 n.32; return to Iraq following second Iraq War, 85; as self-constituted warlord in Northern Iraq, 82; Syrian alliance, 70–71

Taliban. *See* Afghanistan and Afghan War

Tawakalna campaign, 53–54, 55

Tenet, George, 7, 12

Third World Fighters, 119 n.69

Thunder Run, 23

Tikritis, 59, 124 n.37

Tito, Josip Broz, 30

tribal authorities, 57–58, 93, 107. *See also* sectarianism; *specific tribes by name*

Turkey: Assyrian population within, 30; Ataturk, 129 n.30; Baghdad Pact, 29; Kurdish population, 94; proposed invasion of Iraq from, 6–7,

About the Author

STEPHEN C. PELLETIÈRE was the Central Intelligence Agency's senior political analyst on Iraq during the Iran-Iraq War. He is the author of *The Iran-Iraq War: Chaos in a Vacuum* (Praeger, 1992), *Iraq and the International Oil System* (Praeger, 2001), and *America's Oil Wars* (Praeger, 2004).